D1398250

F~OR~ surely He shall deliver thee

from the snare of the fowler and ...

He shall cover thee with his feathers

and under his wings shalt thou trust.

Psalms 90: 3-4

Calvert County Public Library
Twin Beaches Branch
3819 Harbor Road
P.O. Box 910
Chesapeake Beach, MD 20732
410-257-2411

Bitterns

American Bittern

This is a very shy bird. You have to be a bit lucky to see a bittern because it skulks in the tall grasses of swamps and ponds and blends in perfectly. It is so confident of its camouflage that it will almost always freeze when humans approach, remaining still even when they are just a few feet away. By pointing its beak straight up and swaying in perfect rhythm as winds move the grasses, the bittern "disappears."

Vision is limited in the tall grass, so bitterns use their voices to communicate with other bitterns to find a mate. Their call has been compared to the sound of a pump. Another interpretation of the sound resulted in a local nickname, "stake-driver."

▷ This is the famous "bittern stance." The bill is pointed straight up to mimic grassy vegetation. This stance is also used by Green-backed Herons (see p. 20).

Least Bittern

The Least Bittern is even more secretive than the American Bittern and is much smaller. Because of its diminutive size, it is able to climb about on the slender stalks of reeds and cattails. Like its larger cousin, it also freezes when disturbed.

American Bittern

Least Bittern

Least Bittern

Least Bittern

Coot

American Coot

The American Coot is often mistaken for a duck, but is actually a member of the rail family. It has a chunky body and large, lobed feet, which are useful for paddling and running across the surface of ponds to reach takeoff speed.

Coots have a very interesting cooperative behavior. When a predator, such as a hawk, is spotted, coots on a pond form a tight flock and at the last instant, put their white bills very close together, creating a dazzling area of white in contrast with their bunched, black bodies. This spectacle is enough to cause some predators to break off an attack. Ornithology students have demonstrated this behavior by flying hawk-shaped kites over flocks of coots.

Coots are similar in appearance to moorhens, but moorhens have red and yellow bills. However, both coots and moorhens have a "frontal shield," a hard, flat area above their upper bills.

◁ The American Coot can be seen on open ponds and marshes in western New York and Pennsylvania in summer

During winter coots are usually found in coastal areas from Long Island south and are not often seen north of Cape Cod.

A "Raft" of Coots

3

Grebes

Summer Plumage

Pied-billed Grebe

Grebes are small birds found on ponds in summer. They are known for their lightning-quick dives. When frightened, they do not reappear, but may hide among the reeds with all but their bills below the surface. This ability to instantly disappear under water has earned them the names "hell diver" and "water-witch." They have also been called "dabchicks," a corruption of "dipping duck."

Like cormorants, grebes regulate their buoyancy by controlling the air held in their feathers and air sacs.

The grebe builds a floating nest and attaches it to the stems of tall marsh plants. If the female needs to leave her eggs for any reason, she hides her eggs by covering the nest with debris. After they are hatched, the young chicks ride about on their mother's back, covered by her wings, with only their heads sticking out.

"Pied" means multi-colored and refers to the black ring around the grebe's bill, present in summer, which resembles the marking of a Ring-billed Gull (see page 37). Note also the black throat marking. Both the ring around

the bill and the neck marking are absent in winter.

The Pied-billed Grebe is an increasingly rare summer resident throughout the ponds and marshes of the Northeast and can occasionally be seen in winter along the coast south of New England.

▷ The Grebe's bill has small saw-like teeth along its edge which helps it grip its prey.

Winter Plumage
(no ring around bill)

◁ Notice the interesting lobed feet of the grebe. "Lobed" means that the webbing extends around each toe, not between the toes, and each toe remains separate.

The lobes of the grebe's foot aid in swimming in the same manner as the webbing of a duck's foot, but are not as awkward as full webbing. This feature gives the grebe a better grip for climbing around in vegetation.

Pied-billed Grebe on nest with chick

JMWP/VU

Feathers in the Stomach

Scientists frequently study the stomach contents of birds to learn about their food habits. It is not uncommon to find feathers in the stomachs of birds, but the Pied-billed Grebe has the most feathers in its stomach, as much as 50% of the total contents. The purpose of these feathers is to wrap such indigestible food items as fish bones and not allow them to pass into the intestine. The feathers and hard items are regurgitated as firm pellets.

◁ Grebe chicks are transported on the backs of their parents and can hang on tightly enough to remain with the parent even when it dives.

Horned Grebe

Both Horned and Red-necked Grebes are winter residents along coastal waters. The Horned Grebe stays close to shore in bays and rivers while the Red-necked is more likely to be found offshore. The Horned Grebe is a much larger bird. Horned Grebes shed their colorful breeding plumage in late summer and become gray and white for winter.

Horned Grebes are excellent divers and remain underwater for as long as three minutes as they chase fish.

James Bond, Bird Expert

Ian Fleming, the creator of James Bond series of adventure stories, borrowed the name of his most famous character from a world renowned ornithologist. The real James Bond was an authority on the birds of the Carribbean. Fleming, who was a birdwatcher, came across the name in a bird book and found it suitably simple and unromantic, yet very masculine. Fleming offered his apologies for any trouble he may have caused the bird-man. He even offered to let Bond use the name, Ian Fleming, to describe some horribly ugly species of bird, if he felt that revenge was necessary. It seems that Bond was rather pleased with the fictional use of his name and never took up the offer.

Horned Grebe on Nest

JRW/Vireo

Breeding Plumage

Glossy Ibis

Ibises are distinctive for their long, curving bills. Downward curving bills are called "decurved" in scientific language. The Glossy Ibis is found in summer along the coast of New Jersey and in several mixed colonies with herons as far north as southern Maine.

△▽ Notice the variety of colors created as light hits the Glossy Ibis's iridescent plumage from different angles.

The Sacred Ibis

The Egyptians regarded their ibis with reverence because they believed that one of their Gods, Thoth, came to earth on one occasion and assumed the form of an ibis. This is a photo of an ibis statue created by the ancient Egyptians and now on display at the Metropolitan Museum of Art in New York City. It is hollow inside and the body of a real ibis was placed within. Some ancient tombs contained hundreds of mummified ibises.

Winter Plumage

Moorhen

Common Moorhen

Formerly called a gallinule, the moorhen is a duck-like bird frequently seen on freshwater ponds and marshes where it swims with coots (see page 3 for comparison). The red shield on the forehead makes it unmistakably different. It loves to climb around in the tall grasses and reeds at the edges of lakes. It is not common north of Long Island.

Dummy Nests

Some species of Moorhen build a number of nests but deposit their eggs in only one of the nests. Several other species of birds also build multiple nests, most notably the wrens. There are several possible purposes for the extra nests. They may help to confuse predators and are sometimes called "mock nests." Some multiple nests are built by males waiting to find a mate, perhaps in response to hormonal activity and as part of their territorial defense activities. Such nests have been called "cock nests."

▽ Notice the huge feet of this young bird. Moorhen chicks are precocial, meaning that they can move about almost immediately after hatching. They are ready to follow their parents as soon as their feathers are dry.

No Moors in the USA

The common name of this bird was changed from gallinule to moorhen because ornithologists decided the English species of moorhen was the same as our gallinule and agreed to adopt the older name for both even though there are no moors in this country.

Rails

Virginia Rail

Rails are wetland birds which spend their lives in the dense vegetation of marshes and are seldom seen. They have the ability to squeeze through extremely thick vegetation with ease. Birders usually locate them by their voices only.

Although only occasionally seen, rails can be rather indifferent to human observers when caught in the open. Apparently, because their lives are spent in heavy cover, rails are not programmed to be wary or to flee at the slightest hint of danger, like many other birds. Since they are accustomed to being invisible, they tend to carry on with whatever they are doing. They are most active in the twilight hours.

Rails can fly but usually prefer to walk. When they do fly, they dangle their feet beneath them. However, if they are travelling any distance, they stretch their legs straight out behind them and also extend their necks forward. Although reluctant to fly more than a few yards at a time on their home ground, rails do undertake surprising migratory journeys. For example, some Soras winter in Bermuda, a distance of 600 miles from the coast of the United States.

Virginia Rail

Clapper Rail

△ The Virginia Rail can be seen from boardwalks in swampy areas. Early spring is best before the new vegetation becomes too dense.

◁ The Clapper Rail can sometimes be seen in salt marshes at low tide feeding around the clumps of grasses.

King Rail

The King Rail is usually found in fresh water habitats and is the counterpart of the Clapper Rail which is usually found near salt water.

King Rail

Long-billed Rails

Among the three species of rails with long bills, the Virginia Rail is by far the smallest, about half the size of the King or Clapper. The King is usually found in freshwater swamps and marshes while the Clapper prefers the salty or brackish water of tidal flats.

Short-billed Rails

The short-billed rails are called "crakes" and include the Sora, the Yellow, and the tiny Black Rail. They all stay well hidden, but the Sora is much easier to find than the other two.

Birders are eager to spot the Corn Crake, a European rail similar to the Sora which sometimes migrates far off course and winds up on this side of the Atlantic. There have been several sightings of this accidental visitor.

Sora

Sora

It has been reported that Soras are capable of hiding from their predators by grasping reeds to hold themselves underwater and breathing with only their bills above the surface.

Black Rail

The Virginia and Sora Rails are common nesters in New England.

The King and Clapper Rails are uncommon to rare in the Northeast as nesting birds.

Yellow and Black Rails are seen in the Northeast mostly during migration.

Sora chick

Black Rail

This is the smallest of the rails and the most difficult to find, although its *kikky-doo, kikky-doo* call can be heard at night from the salt marshes. Note its red eyes. The white specks on its black back are important for identification because the young of the other rail species are completely black and are sometimes mistaken for Black Rails.

Herons

Tricolored Heron

Audubon called this bird "Lady of the Waters" because of its grace and beauty. The older name, Louisiana Heron, was very misleading. It does occur in Louisiana, but is also found in all the coastal states from Texas to the Northeast. For this reason, the official name is now Tricolored Heron (after its scientific name, *Hydronassa tricolor*).

It somewhat resembles the Great Blue Heron, but it is much smaller and more delicate. Its white belly clearly distinguishes it from all other herons.

The Tricolored Heron fishes by striding briskly through the water, sometimes even running after fish which are caught with a quick thrust of the beak into the water. This move is so fast that it will blur a photograph taken at 1/1,000 second shutter speed. This is really fast considering that a shutter speed of 1/4,000 will stop a bullet.

Breeding plumage

Is this photo upside down?

Note the white patch on lower back

Yellow-crowned Night-Heron

There are two kinds of night-herons in the Northeast: Yellow-crowned, and Black-crowned. The Yellow-crowned is very much a southerner. It is regularly seen from New Jersey south, but is an uncommon visitor to New England.

The Yellow-crowned is distinguished by a white patch on its cheek and a white crown. These white areas leave a band of black through the eyes which gives the bird a raccoon-like facial appearance.

Winter Plumage

Breeding Plumage

Courtship Display

△ This night-heron has raised the feathers on its head as a warning and a threat. This threat is of low intensity as only the plumes on the head are raised. As the threat intensifies, other feathers come into play until the heron is literally bristling with anger.

Night-herons in winter plumage do not have these plumes on their heads, but then they do not have to defend breeding territory and generally just squabble over food.

Night Shift Workers

Like their name implies, night-herons work at night and thus avoid traffic jams with other birds which might be fishing in the same territory.

They must also be workaholics because they are frequently seen in the daytime. However, the tides are more important to these birds than the position of the sun, because they must have shallow water for wading.

Immature

△ In its courtship display, the male Yellow-crowned Night-Heron spreads its wings and makes a dramatic bow toward the female.

◁ Notice the beautiful orange eyes of this immature Yellow-crowned Night-Heron. Compare them to the ruby-red eyes of the adult Black-crowned Night-Herons shown on the following pages.

11

Herons

Black-crowned Night-Heron

The Black-crowned Night-Heron is whitish in the breast area and features a black crown (with white plumes). It is very common worldwide including Asia, Africa and the Pacific, while the Yellow-crowned is only found in the Americas.

Immature in relaxed posture

△ These herons are in the early stages of pair formation. Note the salmon color of their legs during this period.

Notice that the fish-eating Black-crowned Night-Heron has a slightly longer, thinner bill than the Yellow-crowned Night-Heron which uses its heavier bill to crush crustaceans.

△ This immature heron is alarmed. It is in an alert posture with its neck extended and its plumage sleeked (flattened) in preparation for flight.

Feeding posture

Herons

Great Blue Heron

Because of their impressive size, Great Blue Heron are easily noticed and well known to most birders. Their increasing populations are living proof of the value of enforcing bird protection laws. Formerly, Great Blue Heron populations suffered in the Northeast because unsportsmanlike hunters could not resist using the big birds for target practice.

△ This heron is not just "blowing in the wind" but is shaking out its rumpled feathers to align them for flight.

Neck stretched forward for takeoff (over field of loosestrife wildflowers)

WG/Vireo

For herons (and egrets), the head and neck are stretched forward on takeoff, but pulled back into a compact "S" shape and held tightly against the body as soon as cruising speed is reached. Sometimes the head and neck are not retracted at all, if the flight is very short. Many people mistakenly call herons "cranes," but true cranes (and storks), keep their necks extended throughout their flights.

Neck retracted for cruising

LK

RV

◁ This heron can probably swallow its huge fish although occasionally a bird dies from attempting to swallow a fish that is too large.

Herons sometimes spear large fish with their sharp bills, although they usually hold their prey scissors-style. The fish is maneuvered so that it can be swallowed head-first.

Herons

Great Blue Heron nesting colony at sunset.

◁ The touching of bills appeases the aggesssion shown by the raised feathers. Both male and female are equipped with dangerous, dagger-like bills. To avoid bloodshed, the territorial instincts of both birds must be quickly subdued in the initial stages of courtship.

◁ One bird riffles the feathers of the other, a rapid preening-like motion which is part of pair-bonding. The other bird is adjusting twigs in the nest.

△ Parent defending its young birds in their nest.

◁ A mated pair of Great Blue Herons at their nest.

Breeding plumage

Herons

Green-backed Heron

An extraordinary feature of this bird is his ability to contract his neck so much that it appears his head grows directly on his shoulders. Or, he may extend his neck to almost unbelievable lengths.

This stretching motion is probably used to help move a large fish through his digestive tract. It is the bird's equivalent of taking Rolaids. It is known to animal behavior scientists as a "comfort movement."

This is a shy and very low profile bird. It favors swampy areas and the grassy edges of lakes and streams. It occurs throughout much of New England in the summer.

Green-backed Herons are mostly solitary nesters, but sometimes form small colonies.

△ This bird's crest may have been raised agressively in response to the presence of a photographer, a situation with the potential for conflict.

△ This bird is alarmed, but since its feathers are smoothed rather than ruffed, its next move will likely be flight rather than fight.

◁ This Green-backed Heron is seen in a typical feeding posture. It is known for its ability to remain motionless in this position, posing like a statue, for as long as required in order to takes its prey by surprise.

Patience is his virtue and the key to his fishing technique. The Green-backed Heron finds a bank overhanging the water and waits for the right moment to strike. He may also enter the water and stand motionless for many minutes. His bright yellow legs may attract fish.

Fishing with Bait

Green-backed Herons sometimes use brightly colored leaves to attract fish. In parks where people discard food, they have been observed floating crumbs and bits of food on the surface of the water and striking when small fish appear to investigate.

These baby Green-backed Herons are attempting to hide from the photographer by raising their necks, remaining motionless, and pretending to be twigs on the branch.

▷ Note the size of these young birds. They are only about 10 days old and will be completely independent of their parents when they reach 35-40 days.

The bond with the parents is broken when the young birds become too agressive in demanding food. They follow their parents, harassing them and making it difficult for them to fish. By this time the young herons can survive on their own and their parents drive them away.

△ Green-backed Heron on nest.

The Feeding Techniques of Herons and Egrets

1. *Stand and wait.*
2. *Wade or walk slowly*
3. *Disturb and chase (includes open-wing feeding to scare up prey).*

Little Blue Heron

The Little Blue Heron has a remarkable life cycle. It spends the first part of its life as a completely white bird. Then it takes on a mottled color for a short while. Finally, it turns dark blue, the color it retains for the rest of its life.

Look for the bluish beak with the black tip for positive identification.

Dark phase

△ During the breeding season, colours are intensified. Notice the strong blue of this bird's bill and the bare skin around its eyes (lores).

White phase

△ Little Blue Herons seen in the Northeast are nearly always in the "white phase" and are most likely to be seen in late summer or fall.

Kingfisher

Belted Kingfisher

If eternal vigilance is the price of liberty, then, surely, this bird will remain forever free. Of all the birds in this book, the kingfisher gets the prize for general wariness, suspicion, and downright paranoia. The bird watcher who tries to approach this perky species will be treated to a show of tail feathers sandwiched between a pair of pounding wings.

Kingfishers perch on phone wires and branches overlooking water. The kingfisher spots a fish, flies out to a spot directly above its prey, hovers, then plunges straight down into the water. It usually flies back to its perch with a fish in its mouth.

This bird generally fishes alone and is not seen in flocks or even with a mate except during the breeding season. Its territory is usually small and fiercely defended against other kingfishers. Most kingfishers use the same few perches every day.

Immature

Baby Kingfishers

▽ Notice the dark bluish band across the chest from which the "Belted" Kingfisher derives its name. This belt is brown for immatures. Females have a second belt of brownish color across the belly. Both male and female have the showy crest on the head which can be raised when the bird is alarmed.

Female

Male

△ The kingfisher nests by digging a horizontal burrow several feet into the dirt bank of a ditch or stream, and there, in a cave-like environ ment, it raises its young. Depending on the soil type, a burrow can take from a few days to several weeks to dig.

Egrets

Snowy Egret

Snowy Egrets are most commonly seen in coastal marshes. The Snowy Egret feeds with quick sprints through the water to stir up fish. With the prey in sight, it uses lightning-fast jabs to grasp its meal.

The Snowy Egret has extended its range in the Northeast so that it is now breeding in New England and is quite common along the Maine coast.

▷ This is not a tightrope balancing act, but a chase scene. Note the crest of feathers on the head of the bird on the left. It is raised as a threat because the other bird has entered its territory.

The Plume Hunters

Around the turn of the century, the fashion industry was using large quantities of plumes and other bird feathers for ladies' hats and accessories. The demand was so great that the price of plumes rose to over $30 per ounce, more than double the price of gold. The result of this irresistible lure was that hundreds of thousands of birds were slaughtered. The most efficient technique was to harvest the feathers by shooting the birds in their nesting areas. This resulted in the death of the young birds and unhatched eggs as well. Other species that did not produce valuable plumes, but nested in the same areas, were driven off by the carnage. Extinction of many waterbird species was a real threat until federal legislation combined with pressure and money from private groups turned the tide. One Audubon warden guarding a private sanctuary lost his life in the brutal fight. The plume trade was the impetus for the formation of the Audubon societies which then lobbied for protective legislation.

Powderdown

▷ This preening Snowy Egret has white-colored dust on its bill. This is "powderdown" which is spread into the feathers to keep them smooth and aligned.

The powder comes from a patch of special feathers hidden on the breast. The ends of these feathers disintegrate into a talc-like powder. Unlike other feathers, the powderdown feathers grow continuously.

The powder helps to maintain the plumage by preventing matting and adding waterproofing. Powderdown serves much the same function as oil from the oil glands.

Why one leg?

▷ Herons and egrets often stand on just one leg, but only the birds themselves know for sure why they do it. One theory is that tucking a leg up under the feathers helps conserve body heat in cold weather. But if that is the reason, then why do they also do the same thing when the weather is warm? Could it be the force of habit?

Egrets

The "Golden Slippers"

▷ This bird's most striking feature is its beautiful pair of bright yellow feet. The solid black beak is handy for identification if the feet are under water.

▽ This Snowy Egret is performing a courtship display. Note that the bare skin around the beak (lores) which is usually yellow, is now pink. It will turn bright red at the height of the breeding season. Compare this to the green lores of the Great Egret in breeding plumage (see photo on page 27).

△ Breeding plumage includes a snowy crest of feathers on the head as well as fancy feathers on the back.

Egrets

Great Egret

To a novice birder, the various egrets might seem quite similar as they are all long-legged, white birds. For positive identification, check size, leg color, and beak color. The Great Egret is a very large bird which has jet black legs and a yellow beak. The Snowy Egret has telltale yellow feet, black legs, and a black beak with a yellow patch of bare skin in the area of its eyes. The Cattle Egret is much smaller than the Great Egret and is also different from the Snowy Egret because of its yellow bill (which turns reddish-orange during courtship). Finally, there is the confusing Little Blue Heron which is white when immature but dark as an adult.

Open-wing Feeding

Breeding Plumage

Wading & Fishing

Front (fish's view)

Profile (human's view)

◁ During the nesting season, Great Egrets grow long feathers called "aigrettes." These plumes are not tail feathers. They grow from the upper back of the bird. Egrets (and some herons) have a patch of bare skin in front of their eyes (the "lores") which changes color during the breeding season. In Great Egrets it changes from yellow to a beautiful green. In Snowy Egrets, the breeding color of the lores is bright red.

Egrets

Cattle Egrets seldom wade in water like other Egrets, but they have their own unique feeding system. They are most frequently seen in pastures around cattle (thus their name). They follow the animals through the grass. The movement of large beasts stirs up insects which are eaten by the Cattle Egrets.

Cattle Egrets also follow farm machinery for the same purpose. Of all the birds in this book, the Cattle Egret is the least dependent upon water creatures for its food supply.

△ In breeding plumage, the Cattle Egret develops a striking brown buff color on its head, back and the chest.

▷ Note the deformed beak of this bird. Cattle Egets often feed in fields where farmers spray a lot of toxic chemicals, so it is quite possible that this abnormality is a birth defect resulting from genetic damage from pesticides.

Cattle Egrets are seen in the Northeast as far north as Maine in summer. They are found in coastal communities, but not along the coast, as they usually prefer more inland habitats. They are often seen on the median strips of highways where mowers stir up insects.

Conquering the New World

Cattle Egrets are native to Africa and were unknown in the Western Hemisphere until the 1930's, when they suddenly appeared in South America. They had apparently flown across the Atlantic Ocean with the help of strong tail winds. By the 1950's they had appeared in Florida and within twenty years were breeding in Canada and California. This is one of the most explosive expansions of range ever recorded in the bird world. Cattle Egrets are now a common sight throughout most of the eastern United States. Not only did the Cattle Egret conquer the United States, but at the same time spread from Africa to Asia and even into Australia.

There are theories to explain why the Cattle Egret suddenly appeared in the Western Hemisphere. It is possible that the Cattle Egret actually crossed the Atlantic from Africa to South America much earlier, but perhaps there was not enough suitable habitat to allow it to survive and prosper. It was not until recent years that man began raising cattle and clearing heavily forested areas to create fields for grazing. So, earlier appearances of the Cattle Egret could easily have gone unnoticed.

Whether Cattle Egrets have displaced native birds in the United States or simply found their own niche is still under study. However, it is known that Cattle Egrets are now nesting in the same rookeries with other species such as herons and egrets, and wherever they share nesting territory, they wreak havoc by eating the young of their neighbors.

Loons

IJ/Cornell

Common Loon

Loons breed in summer around clear lakes from northern New York through New England and Canada to the edge of the Arctic. In winter, when ice drives them from their freshwater lakes, they move to the salt water of tidal bays, rivers, and the open ocean along the Atlantic coast. When the northern lakes thaw in spring, loons return to their breeding grounds. Their migration can often be observed from Cape Cod.

Like many of the diving birds, loons have legs set far back on their bodies, and their webbed feet serve as efficient propellers. This enables them to pursue and catch fish under water. They are powerful swimmers and can stay submerged for several minutes and cover a hundred yards or more in a single dive (although most dives are shorter).

Loons usually eat small fish but can also take larger prey. A loon will work a large fish with its bill for an hour or more, turning it over and over and crushing it so that it can be swallowed.

SJL

◁ Loons build their nests right at the edge of the water so they can slip off the nest and either dive or swim away from intruders. Nests built on small islands afford protection from predators such as raccoons and foxes and are generally more successful.

Loon chicks take to the water within hours of hatching and when alarmed will crawl up onto their mother's back for a free ride and better protection.

First in Line

This book is arranged alphabetically for easy reference by birders of all levels of expertise, but most technical bird books are arranged in the sequence of scientific classification. Notice that in such books of North American birds, loons come first. In books that cover birds worldwide, loons would be preceded by penguins, tinamous, and ostriches.

Although loons are extremely graceful in the water, they are very clumsy on land and can barely waddle along. It is impossible for them to take off from land. Even from water they have trouble becoming airborne and need lots of open space for a long take-off run. For this reason, they prefer sizable lakes rather than small ponds. Loons do not nest in tidal areas, as the receding tide would leave them stranded and helpless.

Loons often claim and defend one lake as their breeding territory. If the lake is large enough, two or more pairs may take up residence with each pair restricting its activities to its own piece of "turf."

There has been much concern that loon populations are being reduced by man's encroachment into their habitat and by the effects of acid rain on their food supply. The increase of motorboats, with their noise and their wakes, poses a threat to the success of their nesting, and thoughtless people sometimes pursue adults with chicks to the point of exhaustion.

Cry of the Wilderness

The call of the loon is difficult to describe, but it has a haunting quality that is hard to forget. Today there are recordings of loon calls available which give a good representation, but there is no substitute for the real thing. To sit at a campfire by a remote lake in the north woods and hear the call of the loon is one of the ultimate thrills of a wilderness experience.

Winter

△ Loons in their winter plumage are rather drab.

▷ This floating platform is an artificial island constructed as a safe nesting site for loons.

Red-throated Loon

The Red-throated Loon does not nest in the Northeast and is only found here along the coast during migration, more often in fall than spring. It also winters here in small numbers.

Acid Rain

Acid rain is degrading the environment of many lakes in the Northeast and Canada at an alarming rate and threatening the survival of loons, mergansers, and other fish-eating birds. Automobiles and industrial plants are the sources of the problem. Acid rain is caused by the burning of fossil fuels, either petroleum or coal. The gases produced combine with water in the atmosphere to form mild acids which fall as rain. The delicate balance of the environment, once upset, causes a breakdown of the food chain, killing plants, and then fish. Birds which depend on fish to feed themselves and their young cannot survive in these dead lakes.

Osprey

Osprey

The Osprey is a large, fish-eating bird of prey that is frequently mistaken for a Bald Eagle because of its white head. At close range or with binoculars, it can be seen that the Osprey has a dark band across its face and a smaller, less colorful beak than its more famous relative. Even more obvious is the white breast. Eagles are dark underneath.

Ospreys build large nests which they expand and improve year after year. Most nests are built in tall trees, but the Osprey is adaptable and also uses man-made structures such as telephone poles. This bird coexists well with man and seems unconcerned about cars and people.

◁ The Osprey's rough-textured foot is well adapted for grasping slippery prey. The Osprey is the only hawk able to grasp with two toes in front and two in back rather than the usual three toes in front and one in back arrangement.

"Got a Hold On You"

The Osprey plunges feet first into the water and grabs its fish with sharp claws. Sometimes, when a fish is too big to carry, the Osprey is unable to let go. One theory is that the excitement of the catch stimulates a locking mechanism. Some people believe the claws simply sink into bone and get stuck. Whatever the reason, fishermen have caught large fish with Osprey feet attached. These unfortunate birds perished by the same unique ability that enables them to survive.

▽ This bird is lowering its spread wings as a threat. The bird in the adjoining photo is threatening by raising its feathers. Birds often make both threats at the same time. Both gestures make a bird seem larger.

△ This Osprey with a fish is threatening the photographer by raising its feathers.

△ Ospreys can co-exist with humans and make use of man-made structures for nest sites. At right is a platform constructed especially for Ospreys.

△ Osprey returning to nest with fish.

33

Gulls

Laughing Gulls

Laughing Gull

The Laughing Gull is named for its shrill call which is said to resemble an hysterical laugh.

Gull Size

Gulls are not all the same size. Bonaparte's Gull and the Laughing Gull are among the smallest with the Ring-billed Gull the next size larger. Herring Gulls and Great Black-backed Gulls are the jumbo-sized birds. Most gulls tend to flock together in groups of their own kind.

Seagulls?

Scientifically, there is no such species as "seagull" and some dictionaries do not include the word. Nevertheless, it is very commonly used as a catch-all name for the many different kinds of gulls.

The old professor was asked by his students about "Seagulls." Scratching his head he replied, "I don't know about 'C-Gulls' or 'D-Gulls,' but the 'E-Gull' is our national bird."

Laughing Gull

Watch for this!

Gulls open stubborn shellfish by carrying them to great heights and then dropping them. This behavior seems instinctive, but Laughing Gulls do learn by trial and error to drop the shellfish on hard surfaces rather than a soft beach. Herring Gulls will often go through this process many times and then abandon the shells if they do not break open. It is common to see shells on roads and parking lots near the sea-shore where they have been dropped by gulls.

Summer & Winter Plumage

The Laughing Gull and Bonaparte's Gull are part of a group known as "hooded" or "masked" gulls. Their heads are black in summer plumage but molt to white for winter. They are smaller and not nearly so powerfully built as the Herring and Great Black-backed Gulls.

Winter plumage

Summer plumage

△ Laughing Gulls, like most other birds, cannot slurp. They scoop up fresh drinking water using the lower beak like a spoon and swallow by tilting their heads back.

First-Year Plumage

The Laughing Gull reaches its adult plumage after only three years, compared to four years for the Herring Gull. The plumage of the Laughing Gull starts to turn gray in the fall of its first year. If a Laughing Gull has any brown plumage, it means it is still a first-year bird.

▷ This young bird is a few months old and almost completely brown, but gray feathers are starting to appear.

▽ This is still a first-year bird, but probably hatched early in the breeding season, so it is a few months older than the bird at right. The back is now mostly gray, but the wings are still brown.

Juvenal Plumage

First Basic Plumage

The brownish gull above is in-between the down plumage it had as a chick and the first basic plumage, an example of which is shown in the photo at the lower left. Ornithologists call this first appearance of the contour feathers "juvenal plumage." This phrase is not the same as "juvenile plumage" which is often used in reference to any immature bird. The juvenal plumage only lasts for a brief period. See also the photo of the Least Tern in juvenal plumage on page 44.

First-year Laughing Gulls have solid black tail-bands. Second-year Laughing Gulls have mottled tail-bands and the tails of adult Laughing Gulls are solid white. Notice the tails of the gulls in flight on page 36 (middle photo).

Notice the strong color of the soft mouth parts and red eye-ring.

CMG/Cornell

Breeding plumage means reddish legs, a reddish beak, and a red eye-ring.

WDW

Laughing Gull Breeding Plumage

In the breeding season, the red color in the beak intensifies. The eyelids swell and reveal the crimson-red inner flesh (orbital ring) which gives the appearance of an eye-ring. All the fleshy parts of the Laughing Gull become reddish. The red color is even visible in the lining of the mouth.

The distinctive flesh colors of each species may help birds identify each other and prevent interbreeding. The winter plumage of a bird is called its "basic" plumage. The breeding plumage of spring is called its "alternate" plumage.

WDW

△ These Laughing Gulls are feeding on the crest of a wave. They grab tiny fish from the water while in flight but do not dive into the water like terns.

The gull at left is a first-year bird. It has mostly brown plumage and a black tail-band. The two other Laughing Gulls are adults with pure white tails.

◁ Laughing Gull in summer plumage showing its black "hood" and stylish white "eyebrows."

Laughing Gulls may be found along coastal New Jersey and in several isolated colonies from Long Island to Cape Cod and into Maine.

Bonaparte's Gull

This gull was named for Charles Bonaparte, a nephew of Napoleon and a famous ornithologist of the nineteenth century.

Bonaparte's Gull is one of the smallest gulls. In comparison to the Laughing Gull, notice its delicate beak. In winter plumage, Bonaparte's Gull loses its solid black head, but a distinctive, small black marking called an "earspot" appears behind the eye. In the air Bonaparte's Gull shows white wing-tips and a delicate, butterfly-like flight. Look for it along the coast.

Winter plumage

On Nest (Summer plumage)

Winter plumage

Ring-Billed Gull

The Ring-bill is easy to recognize because of the tell-tale black ring around its beak. It is one of the the most common gulls in the Northeast during winter. In summer it is usually seen on inland lakes and rivers, but non-breeders are found along the coast.

The age of a Ring-bill is easy to determine from the color of its bill and legs. For first-year birds it is flesh, for second-year, greenish, and for adults, yellow.

△ Ring-billed Gulls feeding on a freshly ploughed field. Gulls often follow farm machines to feed on the insects which they stir up.

△ Birds sitting on a fence or wire are usually spaced an equal distance apart. This space is determined by the distance they can strike with their bills without changing their position. This separation is called "personal space."

Herring Gull

Herring Gulls feed on just about anything including all kinds of trash and the eggs or young of other birds. They congregate at garbage dumps and fish processing plants where they sometimes become a nuisance. In really bad times they have even been known to eat their own young when no other source of food was available.

First year plumage

Second year plumage

Herring Gull Plumage

The first year Herring Gull is recognized by its dark bill and rich brown colour. By the end of its second year, the bill becomes flesh-colored with a dark tip. Note the gray feathers coming in, also a sign of a second year bird. By the end of the winter of the second year, there will be much more gray on the back. Altogether, the Herring Gull requires four full years to obtain its adult plumage.

△ Herring Gulls have a red spot on the bottom half of their beaks. This serves as a target for the youngsters in the nest to peck at when demanding to be fed. The parent is thus stimulated to regurgitate food.

△ Baby gulls are usually dark and of mottled color to match their rocky breeding grounds. Their plumage changes gradually to gray or off-white over a period of three or four years.

△ The gull at left is attempting a classic fighting technique. It has grabbed its opponent by the bill and is trying to flip it over and peck its unprotected underside. Wing buffeting is also a frequently used weapon in gull fights.

▽ If a gull cannot grasp its opponents bill, it will settle for a wing or any other part.

△ Gulls have webbed feet, like ducks.

A red eye-ring is visible during the breeding season

Great Black-backed Gull

The Great Black-backed Gull is the largest gull in the world. It is a voracious eater and consumes a wide range of food including the chicks of other gulls and seabirds stolen from breeding colonies. Great Black-backed Gulls can kill and eat small puffins and even rabbits.

The Great Black-backed Gull, like its cousin the Herring Gull, also takes four years to acquire its adult plumage. The adult Great Black-backed has a black back and wings with white underparts and tail.

▷ This is a third year Great Black-backed Gull. Notice the black in the tail and remnant of black in the bill, which is lingering from its first year coloration (all black bill).

▷ This Great Black-backed Gull is eating a young Common Tern. Black-backed Gulls terrorize the rookeries of many seabirds.

A Monument to Gulls

The first year the Mormons attempted to settle in Utah in the mid-1800's, their survival was threatened by a horde of locusts (technically, cone-head grasshoppers) which attacked their first crops. At the height of the resulting panic, huge flocks of California Gulls appeared and proceeded to devour the locusts. In memory of this deliverance, the Mormons erected a monument which still stands at Temple Square in Salt Lake City, a pillar with two golden California Gulls.

Terns

Summer

Common Tern

The Common Tern is very similar in appearance to the Arctic Tern. But this is not such a big problem for identification because the Arctic Tern has a limited range in the Northeast.

Although the Arctic Tern does nest as far south as Cape Cod, it is most often found in northern Maine and Canada. It is rarely seen in the Northeast during migration. The reason is that after its breeding season ends in August, the Arctic Tern heads far out to sea for its journey south.

Winter

Summer

△ This Common Tern shows winter plumage. In the summer, the top of the head will become solid black and the beak will be reddish as in the top photo.

Note the black bar on the wing (in winter) which helps distinguish the Common Tern from Forster's Tern (see page 43 for a photo of Forster's Tern).

The Common Tern's impressively long tail-feathers are attractive, but almost proved to be fatal. Early in this century, the Common Tern was hunted for its plumage which was used in the fashion industry. Along with some species of egrets and herons, it faced extinction (see full story, page 25).

Terns

Arctic Tern

Despite its name, the Arctic Tern does not spend a lot of time in the Arctic and many Arctic Terns, such as the ones that breed in New England, never see the Arctic at all. Arctic Terns begin their migration south early and are rarely seen in the Northeast past September.

◁ These Arctic Tern eggs were photographed in a rocky crevice on Machias Seal Island, off the coast of Maine.

Breeding Plumage: A black cap on the head and the bill and legs are reddish color.

Champion of Long Distance Flight

An Arctic Tern holds the world's record for long distance migration, a flight of 11,000 miles from Greenland to South Africa. This flight, although the longest fully documented, is not believed to be unusual, as it is known that Arctic Terns regularly breed at the top of the world inside the Arctic Circle and winter at the bottom of the world from the tips of South America and Africa down to the ice of Antarctica.

An interesting point is that the Arctic Terns which travel the farthest north to breed, also travel the farthest south to winter. The Arctic Terns which breed in Maine winter in South Africa, while the Arctic Terns which breed in the north of Canada winter below the Antarctic Circle at the other end of the world. As they follow the sun, these birds live in perpetual summer and perhaps see more daylight in a year than any of the other creatures.

Black Tern

The Black Tern nests inland away from the coast on fresh water marshes and ponds. It has recently begun to nest throughout most of the Northeast and is common along the coast during migration.

The Black Tern feeds by skimming over water like a swallow to capture aquatic insects, but it also catches insects in the air.

Laughing Gull and Forster's Tern

Home, Sweet Home

Banders working with Arctic Terns on Cape Cod in the 1950's recorded exact locations and installed markers with band numbers showing the spots where Arctic Terns had nested in previous years. These birds showed remarkable ability to return to their exact same nesting place. This is called "site tenacity" in technical language.

One year, a developer paved over some of the nest sites. In the spring, the bander observed an Arctic Tern hovering over the new pavement and used his binoculars to read it's band numbers before it moved on. His records showed that this bird had been hovering over the exact location of its former nest site, which was now covered by a parking lot.

Gulls and Terns Compared

Terns are frequently confused with gulls. Here is a simple way to tell the difference. The Laughing Gull shown in the photo above is a much larger bird than the Forster's Tern. Terns are faster, have forked tails, pointed beaks, and a longer, more streamlined body shape.

Terns swoop down and grab small fish from the water, but seldom sit on the water like gulls.

The swooping flight of the tern has inspired the name "sea swallow" for this graceful bird.

Although it has webbed feet, the tern seldom swims. It will hover in the air for quite some time with its bill pointed down, then dive straight into the water. It grabs the fish and is immediately airborne again. Unlike gulls, terns rarely, if ever, eat garbage.

Identification of Terns

Terns may seem quite similar in appearance, although there are substantial size differences among the different species. In summer, birders usually concentrate on bill color to make their initial identification.

Tern Bill Color:
Least - Yellow (dark tip)
Common - Red (black tip)
Arctic - Red
Roseate - Black (yellow tip)
Forster's -Yellow-orange (black tip)
Royal - Orange
Sandwich - Black (yellow tip)

Terns

Least Tern

Least Terns like to nest on beaches right at the edge of the high tide mark. Violent storms often wash their eggs and young away, but they nest again, sometimes two or three times. The Least Tern is now regarded as a threatened species because of reduced habitat (see box). They have, however, shown an ability to adapt by nesting on gravel roofs of buildings.

Note the white forehead of the Least Tern which contrasts with its black cap and yellow bill (in summer).

△ Least Tern feeding its two chicks which are only hours old.

◁ Least Tern with eggs laid in slight depression on sandy beach.

△ Least Tern with eggs.

△ Least Tern in juvenal plumage.

Endangered Species: Least Tern and Piping Plover

Although they are not closely related, these two birds share a common problem because of where they live. Both birds build their nests by scooping out hollows on exposed sandy beaches. Unfortunately, this is also where humans like to congregate for recreation in the summer.

The natural hazards with which these birds must contend are bad enough. They must face predators such as raccoons and foxes, as well as storms and wind-driven tides.

Attempts to fence off some beaches as reserves have had a little success but the continuing pressure seems likely to doom these two little birds to an unkind fate.

Roseate Tern

The endangered Roseate Tern is very local in the Northeast, being found mostly in two large colonies in Massachusetts and New York. Small numbers are also found nesting in Nova Scotia and on certain islands off the coast of Maine and Massachusetts. They are seldom seen in migration.

There are only a few thousand pairs of Roseate Terns in North America and more than half of these nest in Massachusetts. Other nesting areas include the Dry Torgugas (Florida) and the Virgin Islands.

▷ The name "Roseate" refers to the pinkish tinge sometimes visible on this tern's breast. However, this field mark is very subtle and difficult to observe. In summer this is the only tern with a mostly black bill (the breeding Roseate may show some red near the base of its bill). The rapid, flicking wing-beat of the Roseate in flight is often a helpful clue. Note also the long tail feathers.

Winter Plumage

Royal Tern

These terns have beautiful orange bills and perky looking tufts of black feathers on the back of their heads. Like other terns, they frequently flock together in large groups on sandbars and beaches. They nest no farther north than Maryland, but some do wander up the coast every summer.

Winter Plumage:
No black cap

Sandwich Tern

Once known as Cabot's Tern, this bird is recognized by the yellow at the tip of its bill, which birders call the "mustard on the sandwich." However, it received its name from the location where one of the first specimens was taken, the borough of Sandwich, England. Sandwich Terns sometimes visit southern New England in summer but only nest as far north as southern New Jersey.

Cormorants

Double-crested Cormorant

The cormorant species most often found in the Northeast is the Double-crested Cormorant, so named because of the small tufts of feathers which appear on its head during the breeding season. These are so inconspicuous that they are of little value in identification.

△ Cormorants are very common along waterways where they sit lined up on old docks, piers, and especially channel markers. They love to squabble over choice pilings.

△ Cormorants have hooked beaks which enable them to grasp fish. They do not spear their prey like the sharp-billed herons and egrets.

△ "Cormorant" means "sea crow," a reference to its black plumage. Dark feathers absorb a lot of heat and cormorants keep cool by opening their beaks and fluttering their throat pouches.

In summer the Double-crested Cormorant is found along the entire New England coast and on coastal rivers, but is much less common in winter.

Oriental Slave Labor

In the Far East, the cormorant's fishing ability is harnessed by man. The owner of a flock of cormorants places metal rings around the birds' necks and puts them on leashes. The birds are then released from a small boat and dive to catch fish.

A Link with the Past

Some fishermen in New England refer to cormorants as "shags," which is the name of a European species of cormorant. Through their continuing use of this name, these fishermen may be keeping alive a link with their ancestors from Europe.

Great Comorant on Nest

Why Cormorants Spread Their Wings to Dry

Cormorants have oil glands, like most other water birds, which serve to water-proof their plumage when they preen. But their feathers are modified in such a way that they do not shed water well. Thus, their imperfectly waterproofed plumage becomes wet after underwater fishing. To dry out their plumage, they sit on a perch and spread their wings to catch the rays of the sun. Although wet feathers may be troublesome to dry, they allow cormorants to overcome their buoyancy and chase fish underwater more easily.

Great Cormorant

There is a larger cormorant, the Great Cormorant, which is sometimes seen along the coast, north of Cape Cod, in winter. However, any cormorant seen in the Northeast from April to November is most likely the Double-crested.

The Great Cormorant is distinguished by its white throat and white flank patches.

Skimmer

Black Skimmers

In the Northeast, skimmers nest mostly at the edges of tern colonies on coastal islands or barrier beaches. They return to the same nest sites every year.

△ Dead bird? No, just a Black Skimmer resting on a warm asphalt parking lot.

△ This is what a skimmer's wet tail feathers look like after the bird has been fishing all day.

△ The immature skimmer lacks the jet-black wing feathers of the adult.

◁ This bird is getting too big for the nest, but still wants to hide from the sun under its parent. Skimmers have vertical-slit eye pupils which reduce the harsh glare from the white sand.

Winter Plumage

Why Sanderlings Form Small Flocks

Some birds, such as the Semipalmated Sandpiper, form very large flocks consisting of thousands of birds. But these large flocks are usually found on mudflats where food is abundant. Sanderlings live on beaches and the small amounts of food found on beaches can only support small flocks. So, Sanderlings as a species, balance the benefits of flocking (safety in numbers) against the problem that large numbers could deplete a food supply. For this reason, they form small flocks on the beaches where they spend their winters. Large flocks of Sanderlings are sometimes observed during migration at places like Newburyport Harbor, Massachusetts, but these birds are usually found feeding on tidal flats, not beaches.

Waves Stir Up Food

The sanderling habit of dashing back and forth in front of waves is well known. But if you look closely, what appears to be aimless mob behavior is actually a food-getting strategem that allows Sanderlings to obtain food morsels washed up or uncovered by waves. Sanderlings depend on wave action to bring them food from the sea.

Breeding Plumage

These Sanderlings are foraging for horseshoe crab eggs. Their brownish color is their summer breeding plumage which is only seen in the northeast during their spring and fall migration.

Sandpipers

Winter Plumage

Willet (or won't it)

The Willet stands out on the beach because it is much larger than many of the other sandpipers.

In flight the Willet shows a distinct white stripe on its wings. In summer, a pattern of darker feathers appears on the Willet's chest.

The plumage of the Willet shows flashy contrast when the wings are extended for flight, but is rather somber when the bird is on land. The eye-catching plumage seen in flight may be a "come join me" flocking signal to other Willets. By simply folding its wings against its body, the Willet becomes drab and inconspicuous when this signal is not needed.

Breeding Plumage

Yellowlegs

The yellowlegs is another relatively large sandpiper, but not as large as the Willet. The bright yellow leg color makes identification easy. The bird shown at right is the Greater Yellowlegs. There is also, as you might guess, a Lesser Yellowlegs which is a smaller bird with a shorter beak. The beak of the Lesser is straight. The beak of the Greater is slightly upturned.

Lesser Yellowlegs

Greater Yellowlegs

Dowitchers

The dowitcher looks very much like a snipe, but is more sociable and is often found in the company of other shorebirds, from which it is easily distinguished by its long bill. This bill is very useful for probing deeply into the ground on mudflats and the edges of ponds.

There is a Short-billed Dowitcher, and also a Long-billed Dowitcher. They are hard to tell apart because even the Short-billed Dowitcher has a very long bill. However, the Short-billed is more common in the Northeast. Dowitchers are brownish in the summer, as in the photos, but gray and rather colorless in the winter.

Short-billed Dowitchers

Long-billed Dowitchers

53

Turnstone

Winter plumage

Ruddy Turnstone

The Ruddy Turnstone is well-named. It has a reddish-brown body, red legs, and is known for turning over every stone and shell on the beach in its search for food. It is usually found on the type of beach that has lots of rocks and seaweed. The Ruddy is named for its reddish-brown body color and not for its red legs.

The "Dear Enemy" Phenomenon

Many territorial birds recognize their neighbors by their songs and do not respond to them aggressively. This is called the "dear enemy" phenomenon. Energy is saved by not having to respond to enemies with whom differences have already been settled. Turnstones do not have recognizable songs. However, the pattern of head feathers in turnstones is highly variable, so much so that individual birds can recognize each other by this means. Turnstones quickly learn to recognize their neighbors on the breeding grounds and thus save energy, once territorial boundaries have been established, by only chasing intruders. In winter this recognition ability also helps, as individuals who have aready fought and established a pecking order need not repeat their battles.

Breeding plumage

Dunlin

Summer breeding plumage

Dunlin

The Dunlin in summer plumage has a reddish brown back, a distinctive black patch on the belly, and a long, black beak that turns slightly downward at the tip. After breeding in the Arctic in the summer, the Dunlin winters along the coast from southern Maine southward.

Winter plumage

Breeding plumage

Oystercatcher

American Oystercatcher

The most amazing feature of this bird, of course, is the bright red bill which is flat on both sides and used skillfully to pry open shellfish. It is also poked into the mud to grasp deeply buried prey and can be used to pry free various shellfish that attach themselves to rocks.

The American Oystercatcher nests in the Northeast along the beaches in southern New Jersey, Long Island, and Cape Cod. It doesn't build much of a nest, but lays its eggs in a slight depression. The Oystercatcher puts on a broken wing act to lure animals away from its eggs, which, when left alone, are well camouflaged to resemble the rocky beaches on which they are laid.

"Hello"

"Goodbye"

Knot

Winter Plumage

Red Knot

Knots are known for their long-distance migrations. They breed in the Arctic in the summer and then fly south to areas from Florida to Argentina where they spend the winter. (See page 65 for the fascinating story of how knots manage to find food during this long journey). Although brownish-red in summer, Red Knots are usually seen in the Northeast during migration in spring and fall when they are wearing their drab winter plumage. Knots often flock with dowitchers, shorebirds which are quite similar in appearance during winter. One distinction is that knots have a whitish rump crossed with gray bars while dowitchers have black feathers down the middle of their white rump.

Some birders call Red Knots (and certain other sandpipers) "plumps" because of their short necks and overall thick, well-fed appearance.

Red Knots (in breeding plumage) feeding on the eggs of horshoe crabs

Shorebird and Landbird Migration Compared

Although some landbirds do use staging areas to fatten up before beginning a long migratory journey, most shorebirds routinely use such staging areas both in spring and fall. The migration of shorebirds is often much longer than that of most landbirds. Many shorebirds breed in the arctic and subarctic. These birds must reach their breeding areas as soon as the land is free of snow so that they can complete the nesting cycle in the brief two months or so before the snow returns. The timing of landbird migration is not quite so critical.

Plovers

Black-bellied Plover breeding plumage

Black-bellied Plover

The Black-bellied Plover is a shy bird, quick to take flight when danger threatens. Especially large flocks of Black-bellied Plovers are seen on the Monomoy Islands off Cape Cod every year.

Plovers have short bills which bulge to a slightly greater thickness at the tip. This shape has been compared to that of a pigeon's bill. Plovers flock together with sandpipers. While feeding, they typically run a short distance, look around, pick up food items if available, and then run again.

Drab plumage makes plovers less conspicuous to their enemies during winter when the gaudy breeding plumage is not needed to attract a mate.

Winter plumage

Breeding plumage

Plover Camouflage

Plovers illustrate several important principles of camouflage in nature. One is called protective coloration. The color of the backs of plovers matches their habitat. The light-colored backs of the Piping Plovers match the sand of the beaches where they are usually found. The darker backs of Semipalmated Plovers match the darker color of the wet sand and mud where they usually search for food.

Semipalmated Plover

"Semipalmated" means having incomplete webbing which extends less than halfway to the ends of the toes. Semipalmateds are also called "ring-necks" because of the single black band across their upper breasts. They are found in small flocks along the beaches and are frequently seen sleeping during the day. Sleeping at certain times during the day is a common habit of all shorebirds, especially when their feeding areas are covered by deep water. However, not all the birds in such a flock are sleeping at the same time. There are always some birds which stay alert to warn of danger.

Piping Plover

Note the orange bill with a black tip. The breast band of the female is usually incomplete and is slightly browner than that of the male. The breast band of the male is blackish and may be either a complete or incomplete ring.

Piping Plovers are well camouflaged when viewed against the sand where they forage, searching for small creatures. They are found almost exclusively on beaches.

The Piping Plover breeds on beaches from New England and Long Island south to Maryland. Its nest is just a depression in the sand. The extremely effective camouflage of the Piping Plover may be a disadvantage when the bird is pitted against human beach-goers with their off-the-road vehicles. Now declared an endangered species, conservation efforts are underway throughout its range to improve its breeding success. Volunteers rope off nesting areas in an effort to reduce contact with humans. Other wildlife management techniques help protect breeding birds from predators.

Semipalmated Plover

Piping Plover

Countershading

Semipalmated and Piping Plovers are white underneath, a type of coloration called counter-shading. Strong sunlight tends to lighten the darker color of their backs while the shadow formed under the bird's body is lightened by the white coloration and light reflected from the beach. The result is that in strong sunlight the shadows and highlights that usually reveal the form of an object blend together and the bird becomes harder to see. The black bands across the breasts of plovers in summer plumage are called "disruptive patterns." At a distance, they tend to divide the form of the bird into two shapes, neither of which is bird-like.

Piping Plover

Lesser Golden Plover

Lesser Golden Plover

Formerly called the American Golden Plover, this bird breeds in Canada and winters in South America. It is seen in the Northeast only during migration. Along with the Arctic Tern, the Lesser Golden annually completes one of the longest migrations of any bird.

Least Sandpiper

The Least is the smallest sandpiper in the Northeast. It is recognized by its tiny size and its greenish-yellow legs. It is also more reddish-brown than the other small sandpipers. When faced with danger, Least Sandpipers fly up suddenly and then quickly come together into a tight flock. This flocking behavior is also common to many other shorebirds.

Winter Plumage

Breeding Plumage

"Peeps"

Several species of small sandpipers look very much alike and are found together in large flocks during migration. To identify these is the ultimate test for an expert birder. Most people simply lump them together and call them "peeps." Some of the sandpipers frequently included in this informal classification are the Least, the Semipalmated, the Western, and the White-rumped.

Pectoral Sandpiper

Note the attractive pattern of streaks on the Pectoral's breast which many authors describe as a "bib." It is most evident in the front view where the separation of the streaked breast and pure white belly is clearly defined. Air sacs beneath the breast are inflated during courtship displays. The breeding plumage of the Pectoral Sandpiper is somewhat similar to that of the Least, but the Least is a much smaller bird.

Juvenile

The Pectoral Sandpiper was formerly called a "grass snipe" because it likes meadowlands and marshes. Also, the white lines on the dark-colored back visible in the photos at left are similar to the plumage pattern of a snipe.

Purple Sandpiper

The Purple Sandpiper is found along the rocky shores of New England (only in winter). Farther south, where there are fewer rocks on the beaches, it is only found around rock jetties and breakwaters. It searches the rocks for small shellfish, frequently in the company of turnstones and Sanderlings.

It is usually the only sandpiper seen along the coast of the Northeast during winter. In summer, a few stragglers may remain in the Northeast, but most migrate up to their breeding grounds in the northern tundra.

There is little about this sandpiper that suggests the color purple. It is actually grayish-brown in winter and even more brown in summer. The origin of its name remains a mystery.

Semipalmated Sandpiper

The Semipalmated is one member of a trio of birds that gives fits when it comes to identification. The Least, Western, and Semipalmated are very similar in appearance. The Least is the smallest and has yellow legs. The other two can be distinguished in breeding plumage as the back of the Semipalmated is grayish-brown and streaked while the back of the Western is more reddish and has a V-pattern rather than streaking.

In winter plumage, these two are almost impossible to distinguish. In fact, Audubon and other famous ornithologists of the previous century failed to separate them.

The Meaning of "Semipalmated"

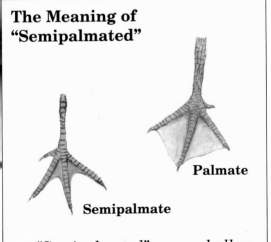

Palmate

Semipalmate

"Semipalmated" means shallow, incomplete webbing between the toes. This feature alone does not guarantee accurate identification as the Western Sandpiper is also semipalmated.

Spotted Sandpiper

Spotted Sandpipers are usually seen alone rather than in flocks and are more common around the inland waters of ponds and streams. While foraging for food and even while standing still, they engage in a tail-bobbing motion called "teetering," and they are sometimes called Teeter-tails. The call of the Spotted Sandpiper is distinctive and is described as a sharp "peet-weet."

The Spotted Sandpiper is one of several sandpipers that nest in the Northeast. It can be found along the coast and along the banks of inland lakes and rivers.

The Spotted Sandpiper is heavily spotted underneath in breeding plumage. In winter plumage, the spots are gone, but notice the wedge of white at the shoulder. The white line above the eye is obvious in summer and winter.

Breeding plumage

Winter plumage

Stilt Sandpiper

The Stilt Sandpiper favors grassy marshes where it probes in mud for small creatures, using its long bill.

Breeding plumage

The black bill droops slightly near the tip. Notice the reddish-brown patch behind the eye.

Solitary Sandpiper

The Solitary Sandpiper's most conspicuous field mark is its clear, white eye-ring. The dark back and the black and white, heavily barred tail-feathers make identification easy, especially if the Solitary in your binoculars spreads its tail. This black and white pattern is still noticeable even when the tail is not spread.

Even more important for identification is the habitat in which the bird is found. The Solitary is usually found along the edges of freshwater ponds, streams, and wet fields. When flushed, the Solitary will fly high, giving a series of high-pitched *tweet* calls.

Although similar to the Lesser Yellowlegs, the Solitary Sandpiper can be distinguished by its greenish-yellow legs (the legs of the Lesser Yellowlegs, not surprisingly, are a much brighter yellow). The immature Solitary has light spots along its dark back.

Upland Sandpiper

The Upland Sandpiper is found in meadows and does not always remain on the ground. It is known to use perches to see above the tall grass and it often sits on fence posts. The distinctively long, slender neck of this sandpiper is topped with a tiny, round head.

Western Sandpiper

Although similar in appearance to the Semipalmated, the Western Sandpiper has a slightly longer bill which is curved downward slightly more at the tip. Large flocks of both Western and Semipalmated Sandpipers have been recorded on Long Island in late August and early September. In winter, Western Sandpipers are seen regularly on the Atlantic coast only as far north as South Carolina, but occasionally they are found in coastal New Jersey and Long Island.

White-rumped Sandpiper

This sandpiper can be seen along the coasts of the Northeast, but is not common. Note that the tips of its wings extend slightly beyond its tail feathers.

Notice also the very fine streaking along its white flanks. The White-rumped is the only sandpiper in North America with this field mark.

The white rump as a field mark is particularly conspicuous in flight.

Shorebird Migration

Most birds migrate and the sheer size of the phenomenon is awesome. Hundreds of millions of birds travel thousands of miles round-trip each year. How they do it is somewhat of a mystery, but it appears to be the result of cues taken from the stars, wind, sun and the magnetic field of the earth. Migration is driven primarily by the quest for food supply rather than relief from cold.

Birders look forward to spring and fall migration because they provide the opportunity to spot many species which are not seen at other times of the year.

Shorebirds in flight

The migration pattern of the Red Knots is of particular interest. In a spring migration that begins, for many, as far south as Tierra del Fuego at the tip of South America and ends in the Arctic, knots are able to time their arrival on the Delaware shore to coincide with the highest tide in May when the horseshoe crabs come ashore to lay their eggs. An amazing alignment of the moon, the tides, and the flight schedule of these birds allows them to feast on these eggs for a brief period before continuing northward. And this is not all. Knots time their migration to coincide with other sources of food at other points along their journey as well. After gorging themselves on horseshoe crab eggs, the knots move on to James Bay in Canada to feed on Macona crabs at just the right time, when the crab population is peaking.

The Delaware Bay is also extremely important as a staging area for the southerly migrations of shorebirds in the fall.

Shorebirds feeding on the eggs of the horseshoe crab

Stilt

Black-necked Stilt

The stilt is amazing for the slenderness of its legs and beak. However, these features give it the advantage of being able to wade and feed in deeper water than a number of other birds that might compete for the same food. Stilts do catch small fish, but the bulk of their diet consists of various water bugs and larvae.

Stilts may be the loudest of all shorebirds. They nest in small colonies, well hidden in brush. If approached when they have young in their nests, they go absolutely crazy. They almost always spot the birder before the birder finds them. The first glimpse a birder gets is usually that of the stilts in the air, flying circles around the intruder, screaming their raucous calls. This behavior can be frustrating to birders because the noise usually scares away all the other birds in the vicinity.

The Black-necked Stilt is a true skyscraper in comparison with most other shorebirds. A full-sized adult may stand over 15 inches tall. In flight, the Black-necked Stilt is a beautiful sight as its bright pink legs stream behind its black and white body like a pair of colorful ribbons.

Curlew

Long-billed Curlew

Any sighting of this western species would surely be a red-letter day for an eastern birder. In addition to the unusually long bill, the astute birder would look for the cinnamon color under the wings visible during flight.

△ Curlews are known for their long, curving bills (which are much longer than those of Whimbrels).

Whimbrel

Whimbrel

Whimbrels are seen along the coast in migration. They travel in small flocks and fly in V-formations. The striped head and long, curved bill are the major field marks.

Although Whimbrels occasionally appear on beaches and mud flats, they usually stay in salt marshes. For this reason, they are not well known to the general public. Birders know where to look for them.

Godwits

Hudsonian Godwit

Godwits are recognized by their large size, long legs, and long, upturned, two-colored bills. Small numbers regularly stop on Monomoy Island (off Cape Cod) during migration and can usually be found in small numbers wherever large concentrations of shorebirds gather. Look for conspicuously taller birds foraging separately or grouped together in sleeping postures.

The name, godwit, may derive from an old English expression, meaning "good creature" and referring to the fact that in the olden days godwits were considered good eating.

Hudsonian Godwit

Hudsonian Godwits are more common, but a few Marbleds are usually seen in any flock of Hudsonians.

Marbled Godwit

The Marbled Godwit is a bit larger and has a longer bill than the Hudsonian. The Marbled has a barred tail while the Hudsonian's is all-black.

Marbled Godwit

Avocet

American Avocet

The Avocet is a western species which occasionally appears in the east in late summer and fall. It is a strikingly attractive bird which may be as tall as 18 inches.

The Avocet sweeps its upturned bill from side-to-side on the bottom of shallow water to stir up insects, shellfish, and seeds.

Male in Breeding Plumage

Female in Winter Plumage

In spring and summer, avocets are a contrast of colors, brown, black and white, but in winter the brown fades to off-white, giving the birds a washed-out appearance.

The avocet, like its close relative, the Black-necked Stilt, is a member of the family *recurvirostridae*, a reflection of its bill-shape which is recurved (meaning curved upwards). Note that the curvatures of avocet bills differ. The bill of the female has a more sharply upcurved shape than that of the male.

The best places to look for avocets are Brigantine National Wildlife Refuge, New Jersey, Parker River National Wildlife Refuge, Massachusetts, and Bombay Hook N.W.R., Delaware.

BANDING

They call it "ringing" in England and "banding" in the United States. Approximately 11 million birds are now wearing metal identification bands on their legs as a result of the work of several thousand active bird banders. Of these, half are government biologists and half are volunteers, most of whom live along the flight paths of migratory birds.

Bird banding is one way an amateur can make a valuable contribution to science. Banding volunteers greatly assist the U.S. Department of the Interior, Fish and Wildlife Service in its studies of bird populations and bird migration.

The accumulated data is also used by government researchers to establish bag limits and restrictions on waterfowl hunting.

Methods of Capture

Mist nets look like large, black hairnets, but are about the size of volleyball nets. They are strung on poles in areas of suitable habitat. When they are in the shade against dark backgrounds, they are nearly invisible. The nets are strung tightly in the horizontal direction but are loose vertically, allowing pockets to form which entangle the birds. According to federal regulations, when the nets are in position they must be checked every hour.

△ Small flocks of shorebirds are captured with nets fired over them from special launchers.

△ Ducks are sometimes lured into traps by spreading a trail of grain on shallow water.

Getting into Banding

Birders often become interested in banding when they tire of listing or merely observing birds and want to make a meaningful contribution to research and conservation. To obtain a license, a would-be bander must be 18 years old, have the knowledge to identify all the common birds in their different seasonal plumages, and must provide references from three well-known birders. He must first apprentice under the supervision of a licensed bander.

To obtain more information, or to participate, contact:

Bird Banding Lab, U.S. Fish and Wildlife Service, Department of the Interior, Laurel, Maryland 20708

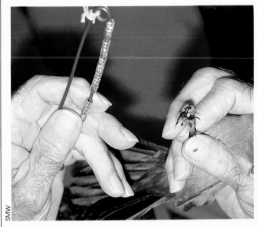

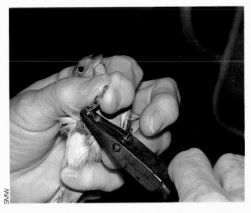

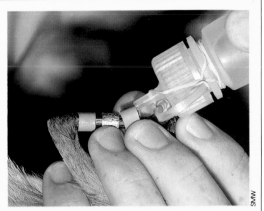

The correct size band is chosen and placed around the bird's leg.

The band is crimped together with a special tool. It is not tight and does not hurt the bird.

An alternative method of banding employs color-coded plastic strips cemented with solvent.

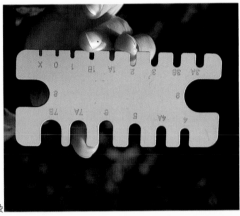

The aluminum bands come in 15 different sizes.

This tool measures leg diameter to determine the proper band size.

Recording the Data

After birds are captured, they are identified. The age, sex, weight, and wing measurements are recorded, numbered aluminum bands are placed on their legs, and the birds are released. The data recorded with each banding is compiled and forwarded to the Bird Banding Laboratory. It is a labor of love, as the volunteers are not paid for this work (but the bands are provided free of charge).

Only about 3% of the bands are ever recovered, but this still amounts to some 40,000 reports per year, enough from which to compile valuable statistics. Unusual finds must be verified because of the possibility of errors or pranks. Plastic neck bands have been used in some studies of Canada Geese.

Recovery of Bands

Bands are usually recovered from birds taken by hunters or from dead birds found along roads or at the seashore. Banded birds frequently show up in the same traps or the traps of other bird banders. If you find a live bird with a band, copy the serial number, but do not remove the band. If the bird is dead, remove the band and flatten it out. Send either the serial number or the band to the Bird Banding Laboratory in Washington, D.C. with the date and location where the bird was found, the condition of the bird, and how it was found. For every report received, the Laboratory will reply with a certificate of appreciation identifying the bird and stating where it was banded. Another letter will be sent to the bander informing him of where his bird was found.

Marsh Ducks

Marsh ducks are surface feeders (dabblers and upenders). They tip their tails into the air and their heads down to feed on shallow bottoms. Most marsh ducks can also graze on land like geese.

Marsh ducks favor shallow water and small ponds because this habitat is better suited to their type of feeding. Marsh ducks leap directly out of the water to begin flight rather than skittering and splashing across the water surface to become airborne.

When viewed on land, the legs of the marsh duck are seen to be centered on its body, whereas the legs are set farther back on diving ducks. In flight, most marsh ducks show a patch of iridescent feathers (called the speculum) which is located along the back edge of the wing and close to the body.

Black Duck

The Black Duck is quite similar to the Mallard and may have evolved from an isolated group of Mallards. Now the opposite is happening. Because of interbreeding, the Black Duck may be disappearing into the much larger Mallard population. Since the Black Duck is prized by

Note variable foot color

hunters and in most cases preferred over the highly regarded Mallards, additional pressure has been brought to bear on the Black Duck population. It is estimated that nearly half of the total Black Duck population is taken by hunters every winter. This is a very high percentage to replace, even in good breeding years.

The Black Duck is not really black but very dark brown, but it may appear black from a distance. Its head is a somewhat lighter shade. Most Black Ducks have red

feet and the Black Duck's scientific name, *Anas rubripes*, means "red foot." However, the color of the foot may also range from brown to black.

Black Ducks are unusual among the ducks, because both the male and female have very similar plumage although the female is not quite as dark. They are also a bit different from other ducks in their mating habits. A Black Duck pair may remain together for several seasons, whereas ducks of most other species find a new mate every spring.

Gadwall

The Gadwall is certainly not a flashy duck in its coloration, and male and female Gadwalls are somewhat similar. Gadwalls are not very numerous in the Northeast and, because of their understated wardrobe, their occasional appearance in the midst of a mixed flock of several species is often overlooked. The male is distinguished by its gray body and black rump (or stern).

Although plumage of the Gadwall is not brilliant, nature has arranged its subtle colors in very attractive patterns that are visible when the bird is viewed at close range.

Male

Male

Female with brood.

Ducks That Cross the Atlantic

Birders are always hoping for sightings of the odd ducks that are far from their usual territories. There have been a number of confirmed sightings in the Northeast of European species, such as the Smew Duck. The southerly migration of birds that normally follow the coastline of Europe begins in regions of the far north. As can be seen from the map, a small error in direction at the start of the trip can become a huge error as the birds progress farther south. Strong winds, often present in the storms of this area, sometimes push birds a bit to the west. The migrating birds may land in Iceland, Greenland, and Newfoundland, and then continue as far south as Nova Scotia, Maine, or even Massachusetts. Asian birds breeding in Northern Siberia sometimes arrive in the United States for the same reason. A small error at the beginning of their journey sends them down the Pacific Coast of Canada and the United States. They may spend their winter in Mexico instead of Korea or Southeast Asia.

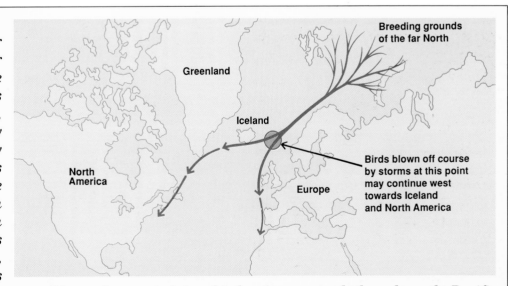

Breeding grounds of the far North

Greenland

Iceland

North America

Europe

Birds blown off course by storms at this point may continue west towards Iceland and North America

Mallard

Mallards are found all across the Northern Hemisphere, including Europe and Asia, and may be the most common duck in the world. They are favored by hunters because they are not only delicious but are also fast in the air and are always challenging targets.

Mallards feed by picking up floating insects and small bits of organic material, such as seeds, from the surface. They also feed by upending and eating weeds and seeds from lake bottoms, as well as grazing on land for roots.

This view of the male Mallard shows the blue speculum feathers of the wings, the white tail feathers, and the white neck-ring.

Is Donald a Mallard?

It is pure speculation, but Donald does have the two up-curled tail feathers that are common only to Mallards. But how could a Mallard be all-white like Donald? Mallards are the forefathers of most of the domestic or barnyard ducks of today, and the color variation of these ducks could include an all-white bird.

Another clue to Donald's species is his loud quack. Mallards, Black Ducks, and Gadwalls are the only ducks that actually quack. Oddly, in the wild it is only the female duck that quacks, but Donald is male and his quacking could be just an unusual characteristic of his domestic subspecies.

Domestic–vs–Wild

Identifying a wild Mallard may not be as easy as expected. Domesticated Mallards are often plentiful in areas where parks or lakes offer a free lunch, but these tame birds cannot be considered on official bird counts. So how does the conscientious birder identify a truly wild Mallard? One useful test is to try to approach as close as possible. Wild ducks are extremely wary and will swim away quickly. If the observer approaches too rapidly, the wild Mallard often takes to the air, quacking. The domestic Mallard often does just the opposite, swimming and even flying toward the human, hoping for a quick handout.

SJL/VU

△ The drake (male) is famous for its brilliant, iridescent green head, yellow bill, and white neck-ring. An interesting detail of the male plumage is the two up-curled tail feathers.

The Speculum

The speculum is a patch of colorful feathers on the inner trailing edge of a duck's wings. Speculum feathers are often iridescent. This plumage is especially common among the marsh ducks. Here, a chick finds momentary shade under its mother's stretched wing.

JHR

The Mallard Complex

In addition to the domestic ducks, a number of wild species have also arisen from Mallards including the Black Duck, the Mottled Duck, and the Mexican Duck. Together, these birds are described as the Mallard Complex. The new species arose as portions of the Mallard population became isolated and developed differently over the course of time through small genetic mutations, the process of natural selection and the survival of the fittest. These isolated populations finally became sufficiently different to be considered separate species.* The Black Duck developed in this manner. This process is called speciation, the creation of a new species. Now, just he opposite is happening. Mallards are interbreeding with Black Ducks and it is believed that in due time the two populations will merge together again as one species.

*Species has been defined as a group of creatures which do not regularly interbreed with other groups. The reason may be physical impossibility, behavioral incompatibility, or geographical or ecological differences. For the ducks of the mallard complex, there was enough genetic similarity that the birds could interbreed, but there was no opportunity for them to do so because they were in different locations during the breeding season.

▷ Bottoms up! These Mallards are foraging on the bottom of shallow water by a method called "tipping." This type of feeding is common among marsh ducks.

Marsh ducks are also known as dabblers. Because they do not dive, they must feed in water shallow enough so that by tipping, they can reach the bottom with their bills.

▽ A raft of male and female Mallards rides in a trough between the waves.

△ Mallard duck in flight.

▷ Mallards foraging in a corn field.

△ Mallards alighting on pond.

◁ Hen mallard with ducklings.

▽ Female with chick on nest.

Mallard Pairs

The mating of Mallards is a far cry from the stately courtship of the ever-faithful swans and geese. Mallards are not monogamous. There is usually a large number of unmated males, and sometimes two males will mate with a single female. Although pairs are formed, promiscuity is common and so is rape. This difference in mating behavior from that of other duck species has been attributed to the fact that Mallards stay in dense groups during their courtship period and there is always a surplus of males.

Common Pintail

The pintail is called a "sprig" by hunters. It has a long neck and an exceptionally long, pointed tail. Note the way the white markings of the neck extend in a thin line into the dark-brown of the head. The long neck of the pintail enables it to feed in deeper water than the other marsh ducks. Pintails spend much of their time tipped up with their heads underwater, foraging on the bottom.

Like the Mallards, pintail females often consort with several different males, and mating can often be observed during the spring migrations to the north as well as at the summer breeding grounds.

After nesting begins, pintail males frequently remain with their females until the chicks have hatched, although the male ducks of many other species abandon the females long before hatching and fly off with other males to a remote area for molting.

This species winters along coastal areas from southern Maine southward. It is a rare breeder in New England.

Female and Male

78

Northern Shoveler

The Northern Shoveler (also called a Spoonbill by hunters) stands out because of its dark green head, white breast and unusually large bill. The broad, spatulate bill is swept from side to side for feeding as the duck swims through the water. The shoveler's tongue pumps water through the sides of the bill to filter food such as small plants and animals from the surface of the water. In shallow water the shoveler feeds with its head immersed as it strains bottom material for small shellfish, aquatic insects, and vegetation. This type of feeding is similar to the system used by the flamingoes and spoonbills of Florida.

Small groups of shovelers may feed together, and it is thought that by stirring the water in one small area, the feeding motion may bring bits of food to the surface. A feeding shoveler is slow but thorough, and very persistent; feeding may continue non-stop for an hour or more at a time.

Male

JRW/Vireo

Male and Female

Shovelers go through impressive courtship rituals during which the male engages in noisy splash-downs. Mock battles between males also occur in which each bird will leap out of the water and over his adversary with a great deal of vigorous flapping and splashing.

The shoveler breeds mostly in Canada but small numbers also breed in some local areas within the Northeastern U.S. It prefers small lakes with lots of reeds and especially likes shallow and even muddy water at the edges of ponds.

Shovelers are not favored by duck hunters. The large proportion of tiny shellfish in their diet produces flesh which is not so tasty to humans.

Shovelers winter along the coast from Long Island southward.

American Wigeon

The American Wigeon is also called the "baldpate" because of the white area on the top of the male's head which gives the appearance of baldness. However, the wigeon is no more bald than the Bald Eagle, and the white is actually white feathers. Wigeons are also recognized by the white patch on the top of their wings (covert feathers) visible during flight, and by their whistling voices.

Wigeons often feed by grazing on grasses in the same manner as geese. Although they do consume aquatic grasses, they also eat grasses growing in meadows and wet fields, especially at night. They return to the safety of the water during the day where they spend the daylight hours sleeping. Feeding is often related to tides.

In midsummer, when the wigeon drakes molt and become flightless for a short period, they are particularly careful to seek the safety of open water during daylight hours.

The wigeon is a wary bird, always ready for flight at the least sign of danger. Because of its acute senses, it often provides a warning to other duck species with whom the wigeon may share a pond.

Wigeons nest on dry land both in grasses and woods. Sometimes their nests are far from the water.

Wigeons spend their winters along the Atlantic coast from Cape Cod southward.

▷ Note that both male and female have a blue bill with black tip.

Male

Male and Female

Male

Juvenile

Green-winged Teal

Teal feed by filtering food from soft mud, so they require a habitat with some very shallow water. Their main source of food is the small seeds of aquatic plants. Teals are known for their synchronized and acrobatic flight. A flock twisting and turning in many directions catches sunlight from different angles and creates a fascinating aerial display. Teals are good eating and difficult targets, so they are highly prized by hunters.

Their plumage is distinguished by a green patch surrounding the eye which is bordered by a thin yellow line. The brilliant green color is visible only when sunlight strikes these feathers at just the right angle. The coloration that gives this duck its common name is the less obvious patch of green in the wing feathers.

Note also the vertical white strip where the breast meets the side flanks. The European Green-winged Teal* has a horizontal white line. Birders eagerly search flocks of Green-wings for birds that have traveled off course, rare vagrants from across the Atlantic Ocean. There are a number of confirmed sightings of such birds, including one shot by a hunter that had been banded in England!

*The European Green-winged Teal was once considered a distinct species but is now considered a subspecies of the Green-winged Teal. So, although such a sighting is interesting and exciting, competitive bird listers can no longer add the European Green-wing to their life lists.

Male

GM

Female

MH/Cornell

△ Notice that the male has a vertical white stripe in front of its wing. It is especially clear in the photo at bottom.

Male

The Earliest Conservation Law?

The Israelites of Biblical times were forbidden to take young birds from a nest and also take their parents. If the young were taken, the parents had to be spared (Deuteronomy 22: 6-7). It may have seemed too unmerciful to take advantage of the parental instincts which prevented a bird from leaving its young and at the same time made it easy prey. But the effect was to conserve species by protecting nesting birds. It was not until 1918 in the United States that the shooting of birds during their breeding season was outlawed.

Blue-winged Teal

The Blue-winged Teal has what birders call a "diagnostic face pattern" because the white, crescent moon marking in the male makes the bird easy to identify at a glance without referring to any other feature. However, the male Blue-wing molts in August and loses its white facial crescent. It may remain in this eclipse plumage until the end of the year and during this period may resemble the female.

Migratory flocks of Blue-wings are usually rather small, and sometimes pairs of ducks migrate all by themselves.

Blue-winged Teals breed in the Northeast. Most winter in South America, although a few linger north as far as Long Island. ▽ Blue-winged Teals in flight show the blue patches on their forewings.

Diving Ducks

Diving ducks are also called sea ducks or bay ducks. They can be found on the open waters of large lakes and rivers as well as bays or the open sea. The legs of the diving duck are set toward the rear of its body, so when it is seen on land it has a much more upright posture than a marsh duck. Having legs set farther back on the body increases kicking power for swimming.

In order to become airborne, diving ducks must run a short distance across the water surface, kicking and splashing all the way.

Male

Common Eider

Eiders are usually seen from autumn to spring floating just offshore in coastal areas of the Northeast from the Chesapeake Bay northward. The females and the brown first-year males may be difficult to identify, but the strong black and white patterns of the adult males stand out. Many eiders do not migrate and remain as permanent residents where conditions are mild.

The Common Eider is found on both sides of the continent. Although somewhat of an academic exercise, the two populations can be distinguished. The male of the western race has a thin black "V" on its throat.

Eiders dive for mussels and crabs. Common Eiders can go as deep as 60

Female

feet while the King Eiders can dive perhaps twice as deep and stay down twice as long, up to 2 minutes. Both eiders also eat rough fare such as sea urchins and sand dollars. Small clams and other shellfish, remarkably, are swallowed whole. Eiders have strong digestive systems which are able to dissolve the shells with acid.

Common Eiders off the coast of Maine

Why Ducks Raft

Diving ducks are often seen swimming in large flocks called "rafts." This is just another form of flocking. The advantage is that through greater numbers, more eyes are available to watch for danger. Also, predators are less likely to attack a mass of birds than an individual bird. The shape of a raft sometimes helps in identifying ducks from a distance. For example, rafts of Redheads tend to be very tightly concentrated whereas scaup tend to spread out and assemble only loosely.

Eider Down

Eiders produce the finest quality down, which is used to make expensive winter clothing, comforters, pillows, and sleeping bags. The scientific name of the eider genus, *Somateria*, means "body of wool."

Eider down is collected from the linings of nests. Each nest can produce about one ounce per season. The down which is gathered is quickly replaced by the nesting eiders, and eider "farmers," mindful of their economic future, make sure that the birds are successful in their breeding efforts. While collecting the down might stress the birds slightly, eiders benefit overall because the eider "farmers" keep watch over the breeding areas for predators such as foxes and provide protection for the birds. Most of the farming is done in Iceland and Greenland. Synthetic fibers have reduced the demand for eider down for all but the finest products.

Eider nest

The breeding habits of eiders are unique in that hatchlings of different females sometimes join together in small flocks and are cared for through the mutual efforts of several mothers. This helps to protect them from their major predator, the Great Black-backed Gull. Large colonies nest on the coastal islands of Maine, where they are isolated from mammal predators.

King Eider

The King Eider is a bit smaller than the Common Eider and has a black back, while the Common has a white back. The King adult male also sports a brightly colored frontal shield, a huge bump or knob, above its bill. The King is a rare find along the East Coast.

Male

Male

Male and Female

Diving Ducks

Two males and a female

Harlequin

Harlequins are known as the ducks of rough water. In summer, these birds dive among the boulders of fast flowing streams. In the winter they head for the seacoast, where they dive through waves around rocks, searching for small shellfish, crustaceans and small fish.

The fancy plumage of the Harlequin is likened to the Wood Duck. The Latin species name, *histrionicus*, means "clown," relating to the Harlequin's gaudy array of colors and markings. Note the circular white patch on the head.

Harlequins nest in the far north.

In winter they are uncommon anywhere in the east and do not range much further south than New York. They can be seen around the Isle au Haut (off the Maine coast) during spring migration. At other times they are a rare prize for even the seasoned birder.

Oldsquaw

The Oldsquaw (sometimes spelled Old Squaw) is also known as the "long-tailed duck." Like the pintail, this duck has exceptionally long, narrow tail feathers. Note also the pink bill and legs. Sometimes, while the Oldsquaw is calling, its tail feathers stand straight up. When landing, the Oldsquaw will point its tail straight down before falling into the water.

Its scientific name, *Clangula hyemalis*, translates as "noisy winter duck," an apt description of a very active bird with a loud, yodeling call. The Oldsquaw has confusing plumage patterns. Consider that the male and female are quite different, and that Oldsquaws have distinctive summer and winter plumages as well as first-year plumage and eclipse plumage. However, the long tail remains a reliable means of identification. Note also that the head always includes both light and dark colors.

Oldsquaws are found farther offshore than other sea ducks, usually out of sight of land, except in winter when they often frequent the shorelines. Because of their capacity for deep dives, they are frequently caught in fishermen's nets. In fact, the marine hazards of oil pollution and fishnets are more of a threat to Oldsquaws than are the guns of hunters.

Male in winter

Male in winter

Scoters

Scoters are found most frequently on salt water. They favor shallow bays where they use their large bills to dig clams out of the mud. Hunters along the New England coast usually call them "sea coots."

The name scoter may come from the word "scoot," meaning to take off quickly. But taking off quickly isn't something that the heavy-bodied scoters can do easily.

Scoters are more easily identified in flight than when they are swimming. Even the experienced birder may have difficulty distinguishing one species from the other when they are bobbing in the water far from shore. Sometimes all three species can be found in the same flock.

Scoter Identification Guide

1. *Black Scoters are all black.*
2. *Surf Scoters have white heads and black wings.*
3. *White-winged Scoters have white on their heads and wings.*

Surf Scoter

A raft of Black Scoters

△ The Black Scoter has the distinction of being the darkest of all the ducks of the Northeast. But, note the orange-yellow knob on its bill.

△ The Surf Scoter is also known as the skunk duck or "skunkhead" due to the white patches on its head. Note also the colorful bill with the distinctive black spot on each side. Surfs are found only in North America, while Black Scoters and White-winged Scoters are wider ranging and are found in Europe and Asia.

White-winged Scoter

△ The White-winged Scoter is so called because of the patch of white on the inner wings visible in flight and often seen when swimming birds stretch their wings. In Great Britain, the White-winged is called a "velvet scoter" after the dull black plumage of the adult male. Note also that the adult males have a white patch around their eyes which is useful for identification if the wings are folded.

Duck vs Ducks

In British bird books, the word "duck" may be singular or plural as in "a flock of duck." The British version of waterfowl is "wildfowl."

The Audubon Society & Ducks Unlimited

Although they arrive at their conclusions from different viewpoints, both Ducks Unlimited and the National Audubon Society agree that serious efforts must be made to protect our threatened waterfowl populations. Ducks Unlimited is a duck hunters' group which endeavors to improve duck habitat in order to produce more ducks and geese for future hunting. Their major thrust has been to acquire and maintain habitat for nesting waterfowl. They are also concerned that the laws governing the hunting of waterfowl be enforced to prevent poaching and other illegal activities. The Audubon Society has a somewhat broader approach, recognizing a need to maintain populations and habitat for all wildlife and to provide adequate habitat for threatened species of plants and animals of all kinds. The original group of interested citizens which formed the Audubon Society were concerned about the exploitation of egrets and herons for the fashion industry, although these birds were of no interest to hunters. Today, the interests of the Audubon Society and Ducks Unlimited run parallel and they often support each other's causes.

In the Northeast, only a few scoters linger into the summer, as they nest farther north. They are regularly seen during winter over the entire east coast, although they are less common farther south and rarely reach Florida.

Male (spring)

Bufflehead

The Bufflehead is easy to recognize since it is mostly black above and white below. The patch of white on the back of the head of the male is positioned so that the entire head appears white when seen from behind. The front of the head is iridescent when it catches the light, but may appear black at a distance.

The Bufflehead is a small duck known for its fast movements. The name may come from "buffalo-head," a reference to the unusually large size of this bird's head in proportion to its body. It has a top-heavy appearance.

When Buffleheads form pairs and head north to their breeding grounds in Canada, it is the females who lead the way, always returning to their places of birth. The breeding territories are spread out and vigorously defended.

Buffleheads nest in the cavities of trees often in the nest holes of Flicker woodpeckers.

Buffleheads do breed in a few local areas of the Northeast, but most travel farther northwest into Canada. Since Buffleheads nest in tree cavities, they usually breed where there are aspens and other softwood trees.

Female

The Lead Shot Issue

In areas where duck hunters are plentiful, hundreds of thousands of lead pellets accumulate on pond bottoms as round after round is fired at ducks year after year. Although some shot sinks into the muck, much of it remains on pond bottoms and is often ingested by bottom-feeding ducks as they scavenge for food. This has resulted in a serious amount of lead poisoning of waterfowl in some areas. Alternative materials such as steel have proven unpopular as substitutes for lead shot because hunters claim they do not have the same stopping power. Although it is generally agreed that a problem exists, there is much disagreement between conservationists and hunters over a possible ban on lead shot. However, bans are currently in effect in certain areas where wildfowl are traditionally heavily hunted.

Canvasback

This largest of the diving ducks is savored by hunters. Long ago, the Canvasback ate wild celery, and even though it was only a small part of its diet, it gave the flesh of this duck a wonderful flavor. The Canvasback's Latin species name, *valisneria*, refers to wild celery. Wild celery is now all but gone due to development and pollution, but the tradition of hunting Canvasbacks lingers, even though the ducks no longer taste the same. For this reason, the Canvasback was vastly overhunted in the 1960's and 70's and is now quite rare in the Northeast.

Canvasback nests are often parasitized by Redhead Ducks. The Redhead Duck may lay one or more eggs in the nest of a Canvasback. The female Canvasback raises the hatchlings as her own. Even more important is the fact that when the extra eggs appear in the nest, the female Canvasback will generally reduce the size of her own clutch.

This pressure, along with loss of wetlands habitat to farming in the northern plains states, plus hunting pressure, has reduced Canvasback populations to dangerously low levels in recent years. But, stringent hunting rules are now allowing populations to grow again.

Male

The red eyes, reddish-brown head, thick neck and delicate pattern and shading of the canvas-colored plumage gives this duck an elegant appearance. Note that the forehead gently slopes into the black bill, giving the Canvasback a distinctive profile similar to that of an eider. The profile of the somewhat similar Redhead is rounder.

Female

MH/Cornell

The female Canvasback is gray in color and lacks the male's white back. A touch of reddish color is sometimes visible on the female's head and neck.

The Family Life of Waterfowl

Geese and swans generally mate for life. At the loss of a spouse, they often do not take a new mate for the rest of the breeding season. Divorce and infidelity are very rare. Among ducks, most species mate for the breeding season only, and although some families migrate together and stay together during the winter, the ducks of most species choose new mates each spring. The females of some species are faithful to the nest site, meaning that they always return to breed at the same location, but they bring a new mate with them each year. Several species of ducks, such as Mallards and Gadwalls, form only the loosest pair bonds. They often seek extramarital affairs if the nesting density is high, that is, if nesting pairs are packed closely together on the breeding grounds, thus presenting the temptation of many females conveniently nearby.

Is there an advantage for survival in the various long and short term periods of sexual fidelity practised by the different waterfowl species? Yes, because small genetic mutations that might carry an advantage for survival are spread faster within a promiscuous population. It is interesting to note that the promiscuous ducks are the species involved in intense competition with other species. Where there is no competition, promiscuity is not an advantage for survival. Among the geese and swans that mate for life, there are few other closely related species of the same size that live together and have the same ecological requirements.

MARRIAGE LICENSE
valid for one season only

Bay Ducks

Common Goldeneye (male)

Common Goldeneye
Barrow's Goldeneye

The goldeneyes feature a white patch in front of the eye. The Common Goldeneye has a black head with green iridescent color, while the Barrow's Goldeneye has purple iridescence. Since the iridescent color is not always clearly visible, note that the two species may be distinguished by the shape of the white patch. It is round or oval-shaped in the Common, and crescent-shaped in Barrow's. In breeding plumage, the bill of the female Barrow's is mostly yellow, while the Common shows yellow just at the tip.

Common Goldeneye (female)

Goldeneyes feed on aquatic creatures, including some prey larger than that eaten by most other ducks, such as small crawfish and mud crabs. Hunters sometimes call goldeneyes "whistlers," because of the whistling sound of their wings in flight.

Goldeneyes have some of the most interesting courtship displays. The most common are tossing the head far back while back-kicking a spray of water into the air, and stretching the head and neck far forward along the surface of the water. Competing males are known to dive underwater and bite their adversaries, sending them airborne. The Common and Barrow's species do mix together during courtship

Barrow's Goldeneye

and sometimes interbreed, but it is not common and there are subtle differences in their courtship displays that probably serve to keep the two species apart.

The Common Goldeneye is a regular winter resident along the New England coast, but the Barrow's Goldeneye is rare.

Redhead

The Redhead closely resembles the Canvasback, and since their habits are similar, they are frequently seen together. Confusion in identification could occur. However, the Canvasback male is much lighter in color on its back and sides. In addition, the Redhead has a round head, while the Canvasback has a sloping forehead and a wedge-shaped head profile. The Canvasback has a black bill, while the bill of the Redhead is light-blue and only black at the tip.

Some female Redheads lay some or all of their eggs in the nests of other ducks, especially Canvasbacks. The host nest could somtimes even be that of another Redhead. This behavior is called parasitizing nests. It is not clear

Male

what survival value this behavior holds for the Redhead species, since not every egg laid in the nest of another duck will receive good care. Actually, the survival rate of such eggs is lower than if the mother cared for them herself.

Ring-necked Duck

Ring-necks are diving ducks but have many of the characteristics of marsh ducks. They can fly without running across the water and feed primarily on vegetarian fare. They are sometimes even seen tipped-up, feeding on shallow, muddy lake bottoms without actually diving.

Ring-necks can be confused with scaups, but the Ring-neck has a black back. Note the white ring around its bill (near the tip) and the white line around the base of the bill.

Why is this duck called "Ring-necked?" Although the ring around the bill is more obvious, the Ring-neck does have a "collar" on its neck. This ring is a dark chestnut color and quite inconspicuous in the field, as it is often hidden by other feathers. It can be seen in a hand-held specimen. The Ring-neck is, in fact, sometimes called the "Ring-billed Duck," because the ring on its bill is so much more prominent.

Rise and Fall of Duck Flocks

Large flocks of ducks congregate in winter for feeding and roosting. One of the advantages of flocking is safety in numbers. A flock has many eyes and ears to sense danger and also, predators are less likely to strike at a group of birds than an individual. However, in spring the flocks break up as the ducks pair off for breeding.

Loafing Grounds

The loafing ground is the place where a male duck spends its time while the female is incubating her eggs. Since the males don't have much to do during this period, they just "hang out." The place for this loafing may be an area of shallow water, so it is sometimes called a "loafing bar." The female joins the male on his loafing grounds for a few hours each day. She does not dare to leave her eggs for much longer. These visits are not for the purpose of sex since the mating period is long past. The true function of these visits in a duck's life cycle is not clear, but in human terms, perhaps companionship is the best explanation.

Greater Scaup
Lesser Scaup

Scaup are sometimes called "blue-bills" or "broadbills" by hunters. They use their wide bills to capture small creatures from the bottom in shallow water. The name "scaup" may come from the old English word "scalp," meaning a raised area of land which is uncovered by water at low tide. Such land is often inhabited by oysters and shellfish, which are the preferred diet of the scaup duck.

Male Greater Scaup

Female Greater Scaup

◁ Note the black-white-black color pattern on the body of the male Greater Scaup.

▽ Lesser Scaup, six males and a female.

Scaup can be recognized by the black markings at both their front and rear ends which are noticeable when they are swimming. According to field guides, the Greater Scaup shows green color in its head, while the head of the Lesser is purplish. But these colors are very subtle and change as the angle of light changes. Most birders tell the two species apart by waiting until the birds stretch their wings. The Lesser Scaup shows white on the trailing edge of its wings close to the body, while the Greater shows the white extending further, almost to the tips of the wings. Greater Scaups prefer salt water. Lesser Scaups prefer fresh water but can be found in salt water also, and the two species are frequently found in the

same flock.

Although most ducks begin courtship during the winter, scaup courtship begins a bit later in March, and really gets under way at stopover points during the spring migration to the north. One reason

is that most scaup males winter in separate locations farther north than the females, so the sexes mostly remain apart during winter.

The chances are that any scaup seen in New England in winter is the Greater.

Male Lesser Scaup

Note smaller bill and peak at back of head.

The World of Decoys

The word "decoy" comes from a Dutch word meaning a trap for ducks. Decoys have been used for thousands of years to lure waterfowl. In 1935 the use of live decoys was outlawed in the US (as was the use of corn for bait). This left the hunter with carved decoys and duck calls for luring flocks. The decoy has recently entered the world of high-priced collecting both as an antique and as a respected art form. The price of a good quality decoy ranges upward from $300 and top carvers get $2,500 and up for their highly detailed and life-like creations.

△ This pair of Hooded Mergansers is an example of flat-bottomed decorative carvings of high quality. They are made from basswood and retail for $1,400.00. The artist is Habbart Dean.

◁ These Canvasbacks are working decoys carved from white pine. Notice the keels underneath which are attached with metal cleats. These particular decoys were used for a season and then offered for sale as decorative items. Each comes with a certificate which indicates the number of ducks bagged over the decoy during the season it was actually in use. The artist is Jim Schmiedlin.

Duck Stamp Millionaires

You can't mail a letter with this stamp, but you better have one if you intend to hunt migratory waterfowl. The duck stamp is evidence that the hunter has paid the fee for his federal hunting license. The federal duck stamp program began in 1934. It was first proposed by political cartoonist and conservationist, Ding Darling, as a permanent source of funds for wetlands conservation that did not depend upon the usual whims of congressional appropriations. This clever idea has raised hundreds of millions of dollars for the purchase and maintenance of wildlife refuges. The act provides that ninety percent of the monies collected be used for refuges and only ten percent for administration. Many states have now have their own duck stamp programs. The winner of the annual federal duck stamp art com-

petition usually becomes quite wealthy. Thousands of artists submit entries every year, but only one winner is chosen in this event which is the only U.S. government sponsored art competition. It is common for the winner to sell reproduction rights to an art print publisher for as much as a million dollars. The publisher then prints up to 25,000 reproductions which will be snapped up by art collectors at a retail price of more than $100 each. Many of these prints are sold through galleries around the country that specialize in selling wildlife art.

Fish Ducks

Mergansers

Mergansers are diving ducks but belong to a subfamily which has special serrated bills (called "sawbills") suited for grasping fish. The name, merganser, comes from a Latin word meaning "diving goose." Most merganser species have crests on their heads which give the birds a sleek, rakish look. The merganser's slender body shape increases its underwater swimming speed.

Mergansers sometimes band together in small groups to chase fish to the shallows where they can be cornered. Mergansers prefer clean water where the fish are more clearly visible.

Hooded Merganser

The Hooded Merganser is smaller than the other merganser species. Its crest, when raised, changes the shape of its head shape dramatically. Note also the two vertical black bars on each side of its body.

Hooded Mergansers, the least numerous of the three species, are rather solitary and don't join together in flocks during the breeding season, but they do flock in fall during migration. They prefer the fresh water of remote, wooded ponds where they usually nest in tree cavities. Hooded Mergansers eat crawfish and insects as well as fish. They are most common in winter from Pennsylvania southward.

Male

Female

▷ After preening their feathers with oil, ducks often shake themselves, then stand up in the water and flap their wings to align their feathers for flight.

Common Merganser

The Common Merganser (called a Goosander in England because of its jumbo size) also has a head crest, but it is so smoothly rounded that it appears to be just part of a large head. The whitish breast and body of the male help distinguish it from the Red-breasted species. The Common Merganser prefers fresh water, but can be found in the brackish water at the mouth of rivers.

Male and Female

Merganser Bills are Different

Except for Mergansers, all ducks, swans, and geese are sieve-billed; that is, they have grooved edges along their bills which help them strain food. Scientifically, these grooves are called lamellae. *In contrast, the merganser bill is serrated, or toothed, and these teeth help the merganser to grasp its fish prey firmly.*

Female Common Merganser

Red-breasted Merganser

The Red-breasted Merganser is easily identified by its long, ragged crest and red bill. Note also the green head, white neck-ring, and brown breast-band.

Red-breasted Mergansers are not tree nesters like the Common and Hooded. Because they can nest on open ground or among rocks and crevices, they are not limited in their breeding grounds to forest areas and they have a considerably wider range than the other two species.

Male Red-breasted Merganser

Female

Common and Red-breasted Mergansers can be found along the coast in the winter months. In the summer, they prefer wooded lakes and ponds in northern New England. The Hooded Merganser likes bottomlands and swamps, but is not seen as frequently. In winter, any mergansers seen on salt water are probably Red-breasted, while those seen on freshwater are probably Common.

Dump Nesting

Sometimes several unpaired Hooded or Common Merganser females will lay their eggs in a single nest-hole and then abandon them. These are females who, for lack of a mate, do not complete the nesting cycle, which includes nest building, incubation, fledging, etc. Their breeding instinct has been aroused to the point that they lay eggs, but that's all. Eggs of other tree-nesting species such as the Goldeneye and Wood Duck may be found piled together with merganser eggs in these nests. The eggs of a dump nest are not incubated and there is no down lining. These infertile eggs are simply abandoned and do not hatch. Dump nests have been discovered with as many as 50 to 60 eggs from several species of ducks piled together.

Perching Ducks

Male

Wood Duck

The brilliantly colored Wood Duck is the only perching duck in the Northeast. It is at home in the branches of trees, unlike most ducks which spend their lives in the water. The Wood Duck can wing through the forest like a songbird. It favors secluded ponds which are surrounded by thick woods rather than open waters, and it is usually found in small groups rather than large flocks.

Wood Ducks nest in the cavities of trees, often taking over the old nests of large woodpeckers (such as the Pileated) and enlarging them further. The nest opening must be large enough for the female, yet too small for a raccoon. More than a dozen eggs are laid and all hatch on the same day or approximately at the same time (synchronous hatching). Nowadays, most Woodies use nesting boxes that have been specially designed and located to attract Wood Ducks.

The Plumage Cycle

After the breeding season is finished, the adult males go to a special gathering place for molting. They lose many feathers and are flightless for a brief time. During this period they are clothed in a rather drab "eclipse" plumage, which serves as camouflage during this period of vulnerability. New feathers are usually in place within a few weeks and the ducks are then ready for their migratory flight south.

Female

Ducks That Nest in Tree Holes

Although the Wood Duck is best known for nesting in trees, other duck species of the Northeast also nest in holes in trees, especially in the abandoned and rotting nest holes of woodpeckers (which must be enlarged). These tree-nesting ducks include the Bufflehead and the closely related Goldeneye species, plus the Common and Hooded Mergansers. Scientifically, they are called "cavity-nesters," and most make use of cavities other than tree holes (such as man-made nesting boxes) if available.

The Big Leap

The chicks are coaxed out of the nest usually within a day of hatching. Remarkably, the tiny chicks jump from the nest hole and fall considerable distances to the ground without injury. They are then immediately led to the water by their mother.

△ Newly hatched Wood Duck chick.

△ A Wood Duck chick leaving its nest box.

Mated pair

The Asian Connection

The Wood Duck is a close relative of the Mandarin Duck of Asia, a bird which is highly regarded in oriental folklore as a symbol of marital fidelity. The Wood Duck is also known for its attentiveness to its mate, and mated Wood Ducks are seldom far apart from each other. Their monogamy is the temporary kind, however, as they find new mates each season. Sometimes a male will father a second clutch with a different female even within the same season!

Stiff-tailed Ducks

Male

These ducks have special stiff tail feathers which are used like a rudder in the water. Stiff-tailed ducks are rarely seen on land. They feed on plants, insects, and small animals near the surface of the water.

Ruddy Duck

The Ruddy Duck is the only member of the subfamily of stiff-tailed ducks found in the Northeast. It is known by its black "cap" and the striking blue color of its bill, which is dramatized by the bill's broad, flat shape. Ruddy Ducks cannot walk on land because their huge webbed feet are set so far back on their bodies. The long tails of the ruddy males are often held up at a sharp angle above the water, revealing contrasting white plumage underneath.

Ruddy Ducks feed on plants, insect larvae, and small creatures found on the bottoms of shallow ponds and bays in winter.

▷ Compare the Ruddy's blue bill to that of the American Wigeon (p. 80). The Ruddy's is much brighter.

◁ The Ruddy's tail is frequently pointed skyward during courtship

◁ Male Ruddy Duck in winter plumage. Ruddy Ducks ride quite low in the water compared to most other ducks. "Ruddy" refers to the color of the male's breeding plumage.

◁ Note the dark lines across the cheek which distinguish this female Ruddy Duck from the male in winter plumage.

Ruddy Ducks are found only in a few spots locally in the summer. In winter they are found in coastal areas from Cape Cod southward.

The Burping Duck

During courtship displays, the male ruddy inflates an air sack in its throat and uses this sack to make drumming noises for the female, all the while forcing air from its wings feathers to provide a show of bubbles in the water. Finally, the bill is opened and the air in the sack is released with a soft, belching sound.

Geese

Geese are generally larger than ducks and most feed on land as well as water. They have longer necks and thicker bills than ducks and the sexes are similar in appearance.

Brant

The Brant is distinguished from the Canada Goose because its black neck color extends down onto its breast, below the waterline, when the bird is swimming. Also, the white chin of the Canada Goose is absent and in its place are a few flecks of white farther down the Brant's neck. The Brant is a very small goose, similar in size to a large duck.

The name, Brant, comes from a German word meaning "burnt," a reference to its dark feathers.

There are two races of Brant in North America, and the race found in the Northeast is lighter in color. Brant are seldom found in fresh water. They breed on islands in the far north of Canada and winter along the Atlantic Coast. Their food consists of several varieties of seaweed or marine algae. But they are particularly dependent on eelgrass, a flowering plant of the pondweed family which grows in shallow tidal sand and mudflats.

In the 1930's a disease wiped out the watergrasses which were the major source of food for Brant. Since then, Brant populations have never grown to large numbers.

Brigantine National Wildlife Refuge in New Jersey is one of the best places to find this species. Look for them in winter.

Why Geese Develop Subspecies

There are a number of possible reasons why geese tend to develop subspecies while ducks generally do not. Most ducks take a new mate every season, thereby mixing genes more widely. Furthermore, the new mates that ducks encounter in their winter quarters quite likely migrated south from widely separated summer breeding areas in the North.

Geese tend to stay together in family groups during migration. The young geese then mate for life with other geese from the same breeding area. Thus, inbreeding is common and the small regional differences that develop are reinforced.

Snow Goose

Snow Geese breed in the far north of Canada and appear at the St. Lawrence River near Quebec in spring and fall.

Their main wintering grounds in the Northeast are at Chincoteague Bay in Maryland and Bombay Hook National Wildlife Refuge in Delaware. Many Snow Geese fly farther south to winter in North Carolina and around the Texas gulf coast.

Snow Geese breed in large, dense colonies which give some protection against foxes and other predators of the far north. Male Snow Geese are aggressive enough to repel small predators on land. Airborne threats to the chicks from seabirds are minimized because most of the eggs hatch at the same time, so there is only a brief period during which the chicks are small enough to be prey for large seabirds.

Note the black-tipped wings

The Blue Goose

The plumage of the Snow Goose may be white or dark. The dark bird is called a "Blue Goose," although it is mostly dark gray or brownish with some blue in the wings. The Blue Goose was once thought to be a separate species but is now known to be a color form of the Snow Goose. Dark and white Snow Geese can interbreed and produce offspring that have light-gray backs and wings. However, interbreeding is not common as the Snow Goose prefers to mate with birds of its own color.

White form and the "Blue Goose"

Keep on Smiling

The dark area between the upper and lower beak of the Snow Goose is filled with lamellae, parallel plates used to filter out food like the baleen of a whale. Birders refer to this area as the "smile." Ornithologists call it a "grin-patch."

If you see a small "snow goose" without a smile, it is probably the much rarer Ross's Goose. Snow and Ross's Geese are often seen together and a large flock of Snow Geese is likely to contain a few Ross's Geese. Birders sometimes scan flocks of Snow Geese with spotting scopes in hopes of finding birds of the rarer species.

The overwhelming majority of Snow Geese in the eastern flyway are the pure white form (with contrasting black wing tips).

To see a flock of several thousand geese rise from a marsh in formation is one of the real thrills of birding. To hear the sounds of such a flock for the first time is an unforgettable experience with noise so loud as to make the usual words of astonishment unheard.

The yellowish color which is sometimes seen on the heads of Snow Geese is a ferrous stain that appears after the birds have been feeding on roots in iron-rich soils.

All About Those V-Shaped Flight Formations

Birds flying in V-shaped flocks are not, as many people believe, following a dominant bird who is their leader. Rather, it is a case of following the course of the least resistance. In any group, one bird must be ahead of the others. The others follow whoever is at the front because the wings of the lead bird create circular vortices of air and an updraft which gives a lift to the bird just behind each wing-tip. It is this updraft that aids the trailing birds, not a slipstream which cuts wind resistance (such as auto racers use when they "draft" the car ahead of them). Flight is more tiring for the lead bird and he will soon drop

back. The V-shape will change to a W-shape, the birds will re-group, and a new leader will take over for a short while. These fascinating long lines of waterfowl in flight are called "skeins."

The V-shaped flight pattern is common to large, heavy birds with

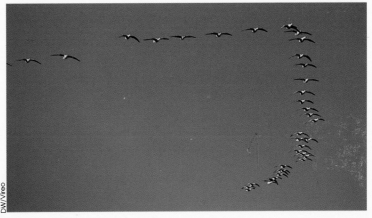

broad wings, such as cormorants, geese, swans, and large ducks. These birds receive the most benefits from formation flying because body weight is large in relation to their wing area (this ratio is known as "wing load"). The energy saved by formation flying allows the birds that possess this behavior to arrive at their breeding grounds earlier (thus allowing their young to fledge before the storms of winter) and healthier (thus making them less vulnerable to diseases and to predators).

Canada Goose

The Canada Goose is recognized by its black head and neck with white "chinstrap," plus the buff-colored breast feathers which distinguish it from the Brant. The Canada Goose is also known for its deep, distinctive honking voice.

Not all Canada Geese are from Canada

Throughout the Northeast today, there are wild populations of Canada Geese which are basically permanent residents. Many flocks have been subsidized by an adoring public. In some areas they have prospered and multiplied to the point of becoming first-rate nuisances.

Golf Ball Goose

Notice the golf ball in this nest. Canada Geese frequently nest near golf courses. They are grazers and like the open grass. Canada Geese will pick up any egg-like object within a few feet of their nests and brood it as if it was one of their own eggs. However, in this particular case, the golf ball may have been placed in the nest by a prankster.

Most songbirds can tell the difference between their own egg and an object resembling an egg or their own egg and the egg of another bird. Those that cannot may become victims of nest parasitizers such as the cowbird (see page 13, **Birds of the Northeast**). But geese and most species of ducks have never been seriously threatened by nest parasitizers, so they have not developed, through natural selection, the ability to recognize their own eggs.

(see page 13, **Birds of the Northeast**)

Many Races

Canada Geese vary considerably across the United States from large and pale to small and dark. They have been divided into eleven races. The "Atlantic" is the most common race in the Northeast.

Why so many Goslings?

Canada Geese sometimes engage in kidnapping (forced adoption) of goslings, especially where there is overcrowding. The dominant female of an area may take goslings from their parents, so it is not uncommon to see a pair of Canada Geese with one or two goslings and another pair with twenty or more, although the average clutch is seven or eight. These kidnapped goslings may have a higher survival rate. They are less vulnerable to predators while living in the center of a large group, the premier territory usually occupied by a dominant female.

◁ Canada Geese graze on land as well as water and can eat plants, their seeds, and roots. They stop many times to eat and gain weight during their journey north. This piecemeal migration is unusual as most other species fly non-stop. Canada Geese breed earlier and farther north. They must arrive fat because their food supply is limited until later in the season.

Families That Stay Together

During their annual migrations south, Canada Goose parents and their young travel together and stay together as a family through the winter. When it is time for breeding in the spring the young birds form together in non-breeding flocks. They do not breed until their third year and are no longer welcome to join their parents.

Swans

Mute Swan

The Mute Swan is distinguished by its curved neck and the way it raises its wings like sails as it swims. The raised wings are not just a beautiful pose, like a ballet dancer waltzing across a stage. They are a threatening gesture and a sign of belligerence which is called "busking."

Mute Swans are not actually mute. They can make a variety of noises but do not have the loud calls of other swan species.

△ The limber neck of the Mute Swan is twisted into pretzel-like shapes as the bird preens itself.

▷ When two Mute Swans approach each other, their graceful necks usually form a romantic outline of a heart.

◁ The Mute Swan's large, webbed foot is a powerful paddle under the water.

The Queen's Swan

Historically, no commoner could shoot a swan. They were all owned by royalty and only royalty could possess them to grace their lavish homes or dinner tables. To this day in England, there is still a Royal Keeper of the Swans.

The Mute Swan is the swan most commonly seen in public parks in the United States. It was introduced to this country from Europe early in this century as a decoration for the homes of wealthy people in Rhode Island and eastern Connecticut who admired and wished to imitate the lifestyles of European royalty.

Affluent towns such as Newport and Watch Hill were the main places of introduction, and although Mute Swans have spread up and down the coast of the Northeast, their core population is still in this area. The Coast Guard Academy in New London, Connecticut, has a flock on the adjoining Thames River. In some parts of New York, Long Island and the Connecticut shore, wild populations have become established in recent years.

Compared to the female, the male Mute Swan has a larger black "knob" above its orange bill and a somewhat larger overall size. During the breeding season, the male Mute Swan becomes quite aggressive and will attack any creature (including a human) which it considers to be an intruder.

Mute Swans do not migrate and usually stay in the same general area for their entire lives. They eat plants growing on the bottom of ponds. Because of their long necks, they can usually reach their food without tipping up, although they may be seen tipping occasionally.

◁ This alert posture is the first stage of a low intensity threat display.

107

Tundra Swan

Tundra Swans are so called because they breed in the tundra of the far north. Until recently, they were called Whistling Swans. They do not actually whistle although they do have a loud, sharp call.

Tundra Swans mate for life, and if a mate dies, often years pass before a new mate is taken. The divorce rate is almost nil.

Tundra Swans have a long breeding period. For this reason, they usually arrive at their breeding grounds in the extreme north of Canada and begin breeding while ice is still on the ground, in order to leave with their offspring before the winter storms begin.

▷ Note the patch of yellow on the Tundra Swan's black beak just behind the nostrils.

Swan Songs

The expression, "swan song," meaning a final act or final appearance, is said to come from the beautiful song sung by a dying swan. Some say that dying swans do not sing, but other observers claim that a swan that has been shot in flight sometimes produces one long note as it exhales its last breath on its way to the ground. The Tundra Swan has been the source of some of these stories.

Why the Name Was Changed

The "Whistling" Swan of the Americas and the "Bewick's Swan" (pronounced "buick") of Europe are considered subspecies of the same species. The American Ornithological Union (AOU), in an attempt to unify terms with its British counterpart (BOU), agreed to call the species Tundra Swan since both subspecies breed in Arctic tundra regions. A similar cooperative effort occurred when the Common Gallinule was recently renamed, adopting the British name of Common Moorhen.

In the Northeast, Tundra Swans are found on the Chesapeake Bay where they seek winter refugee from the cold of northeast Canada. They concentrate in a small area off the upper bay between Ellston and Annapolis.

SEABIRDS

Introduction to Seabirds

Seabirds feed offshore and spend most of their lives offshore, but all seabird species must come to land to breed. Although the dividing line between seabirds and shorebirds is not distinct, there are some striking differences. Seabirds breed in large communal colonies. At the end of the breeding season some seabirds disperse over the vast ocean and seem to wander rather than migrate, with no specific destination, although they do favor warmer waters. In contrast, others move only a few hundred miles to traditional wintering sites.

Because most seabirds are clumsy on land, they generally nest on offshore islands where there is some isolation and protection from mammalian predators (including man). Their nests are crowded together, again for protection, especially from birds that might prey on both eggs and young. One can sometimes observe gulls stalking around the perimeter of such a colony, waiting for a chance to rush in and raid a nest while the parents are out feeding.

Crowded conditions seem to provide sexual stimulation which does not exist when seabirds are isolated, so breeding success depends upon having a large number of nesting pairs. This is a psychological factor which is not clearly understood.

The seabird islands, with their high, rocky cliffs, also provide updrafts which are of critical importance. There are two types of seabirds and both depend upon constant wind. The first type is equipped to soar aloft for long periods and must have winds to ride. The other type of seabird is a poor flyer and to become airborne needs either a strong wind or a high cliff from which to jump.

Male and female seabirds are usually very similar in appearance. With only a few exceptions, seabirds mate for life.

Note: A number of ducks may be classified as seabirds, but in this book, the sea ducks are covered in the duck section.

Gannets nesting on the cliff ledges on one of the seabird islands

The Major Seabird Groups of the Northeast

- ALCIDS (AUKS): Murre, Razorbill, Dovekie, Guillemot, Puffin
- TUBENOSES: Shearwater, Storm-Petrel
- BOOBIES: Gannet (The only member of this tropical family in the Northeast)
- CORMORANTS: (covered in an earlier section of this book; some nest on inland lakes)
- GULL and TERNS: (covered in another section; great variation in habitat among the different species)
- DUCKS: (covered in another section; only a few oceanic species)
- PHALAROPES: Red and Northern (covered in another section)

Seabird vs. Shorebirds

The word "seabird" and "shorebird" are both generalizations, and there is considerable overlap in habitat between the two groups. For example gulls are considered shorebirds, but one of the gulls, the Black-legged Kittiwake, is seldom seen near shore except when driven in by storms. It is truly a seabird.

Even more confusing is the use of the terms "oceanic" and "pelagic." These words are sometimes used interchangeably. However, technically speaking, oceanic refers to all areas of the ocean, even those near land, and pelagic means the open sea, far from any shore.

Gannet

Northern Gannet

"Gannet" comes from a German word for goose, and the gannet is indeed a large, goose-sized bird with a six foot wingspan. Gannets dive from considerable heights to catch fish in a manner similar to terns. Gannets have a distinctive, stream-lined shape that has been likened to a cigar or torpedo in outline. Their large beaks and pointed wings are also distinctive. Note the yellow coloring in the head.

The Guano Trade

In the days of sailing ships, vessels often stopped at islands off the coast of Peru to pick up loads of guano, the accumulated droppings of seabirds. These islands almost never had any rain, so the droppings accumulated in great quantity. Since gauno made excellent fertilizer, it was a valuable commodity. Similar quantities of guano are produced at the island breeding colonies off the coast of New England, except that rain washes the guano into the sea. But its benefits are not lost because it provides food for plankton, thus helping to make the waters off the New England coast such rich fishing grounds.

Gannets nest on cliffs along the lower St. Lawrence River and off Newfoundland. The best known colony is on Bonaventure Island on the Atlantic coast off the Gaspé Peninsula. They migrate offshore all along the Atlantic coast and can frequently be seen from shore with binoculars. Any large bird seen diving into offshore waters is most likely a gannet.

△ The birds in the top photo are preening each other's feathers (allopreening), an activity which strengthens their pair bond.

△ The birds in the photo above are billing, another pair-bonding activity.

Gannet rookery at Cape St. Mary.

Gathering nesting material.

Gannets in flight show their highly streamlined shape.

△ These gannets are swimming with their heads under water, looking for fish.

◁ Visitor's must try not to stray from the narrow foot paths on this island, because the landscape is pockmarked with the active burrows of puffins. A careless footstep could expose baby puffins to the circling gulls which are always overhead.

111

Auks

Introduction To Auks

Auks have been called the "penguins" of the northern hemisphere. Even though auks and penguins developed completely independently of each other, the oceans of the far north and the far south are very much alike, and auks occupy the same ecological niche in the northern hemisphere as that of penguins in the southern hemisphere.

Auks stand upright on land like penguins, but unlike penguins they can fly.* Like the penguins, auks dive for fish and use their stubby wings for propulsion under water, whereas most other seabirds swim primarily with their webbed feet. Scientifically, the auks are called "alcids." Their similar, but distinctive plumages are all variations on the same theme: black above and white below.

Auks, like most seabirds, mate for life, and if they are lucky their lives may be very long, up to twenty years or more. Pairs do not stay together all year, but separate after breeding and may join different flocks for migration. They are loyal to a certain nest site, however, and this allows mated pairs to find each other again when the breeding season begins. Compare this breeding behavior to that of most ducks in which the female returns to the same nest site every year, but each time with a different mate!

*The Great Auk, which is now extinct, could not fly and was the most penguin-like of the auks.

Razorbills

Razorbills are readily distinguished from the other auks by their thick bills which are marked with vertical white lines. Their black backs with tiny white wing borders and white front give these birds the appearance of being dressed for a formal dinner. With the exception of two small colonies in the Gulf of Maine, they nest along the lower St. Lawrence and off the coasts of Labrador and Newfoundland. They are occasionally seen off the coast of New England in winter. On the water they can be recognized by their pointed tails which are often tilted skyward.

Notice the white markings of the Razorbill's bill and wing. Immature Razorbills lack the white bill markings.

Black Guillemot

Black Guillemots are the most common of the alcids in New England. They nest on the rocky islands off the coast of Maine and northward into Canada. They build their nest deep in crevices between boulders where they are protected from marauding gulls. The colonies are quite small, perhaps because of the limited number of suitable nest sites on each island.

In summer guillemots are entirely black except for a white patch on the wing. The feet and the inside lining of the mouth are bright red. In winter, they retain the white wing patch, but the rest of the plumage becomes a salt and pepper gray. They have a habit of dipping their bills in the water which is quite characteristic and helps with identification. Some guillemots linger quite late in the fall, but by winter most of them are far offshore. Their favorite food is the small gunnel fish or red rock eel which they catch by diving around the kelp beds near shore.

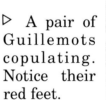

◁ Guillemots in flight show their white wing patches.

▷ A pair of Guillemots copulating. Notice their red feet.

How Birds Chew Without Teeth

All birds have two chambers in their stomachs. The first chamber digests with acid and the second chamber, the gizzard, digests with muscle power. Many birds collect and swallow small stones or coarse sand. In the gizzard, strong muscles crush food against these hard materials. The gizzard of a Wood Duck can crush an acorn and the gizzard of some of the diving ducks can crush hard shellfish such as mussels.

Depending on their diets, some birds depend more heavily on their gizzards for digestion than others. A bird that eats beetles or shellfish or hard seeds requires a larger gizzard than a bird that eats mosquitos or berries.

Seabird Colonies: Sharing the Limited Space

Each species of seabird has its own peculiar requirements for nesting space, so several species can co-exist on the same rocky cliff without competition.

Guillemots like exposed ledges. Razorbills prefer sheltered ledges. Puffins nest in burrows above the rocky cliffs. Storm-Petrels and shearwaters dig burrows, use crevices, and tend to arrive and depart only at night to avoid birds of prey.

Reading the "Auk"

The American Ornithologist's Union (AOU), the foremost American scientific bird organization, publishes a rather technical journal called "The Auk." The extinct Great Auk is featured on its cover.

Common Murre
Thick-billed Murre

The name "murre" rhymes with "purr" and might refer to the purring sound which the bird makes, although the origin of this name is not clear.

A portion of the population of Common Murres (perhaps 25%) has a white eye-ring with a short white line extending backward from eye ring. This is not a different species but simply a different color form, called a "Ringed Murre" or a "Bridled Murre."

Murres build no nests and lay their eggs directly on the rocky cliff ledges. Murre eggs have a tremendous variety of color and markings. This helps parents recognize their own eggs in the tightly packed colony. Individual chicks are recognized by voice.

By banding together so closely for breeding, not only do the murres save precious space, they also defend against gulls and other predators of their eggs and their young. A group of murres will press together along the rocky ledge and strike out with their sharp beaks against an attacking gull.

The two murre species are usually found together on the same ledges (as in the top photo). The Thick-billed Murres do actually have thicker bills, but the easiest way to identify them is by the white mark on their bills.

△ Notice that nesting murres face in toward the rocky cliff. They must. The reason is that the ledges are very narrow, and the feet of murres are set far back on their bodies. Murres bend forward slightly to incubate their eggs. If they faced outward, not only would their eggs be exposed to a fall, but the birds would be hanging over the ledge.

Thick-billed Murres

"Bridled Murre"

Color Forms

Common Murres may or may not have the white "bridle" markings around their eyes yet both forms are members of the same species and may interbreed. Many other species of birds appear in distinctly different forms and the differences within some species are much more dramatic than those of the Common Murres.

Species which have different color forms are called polymorphic and the different color forms are called "color morphs." Here is one theory why this occurs. Genetic material may be damaged, perhaps by radiation entering the earth's atmosphere, causing a gene responsible for plumage color to mutate, or change. If the new color thus produced has an advantage for survival, birds with the new plumage will prosper and tend to replace other color forms in the population. However, this replacement may take a very long time and there may be periods when the changing population includes several different color forms. If the change does not offer an advantage to the species over the old form but no disadvantages either, then the two forms may co-exist forever within the population. This appears to be the case with the "bridled" and "black" forms of the Common Murre discussed above.

Dovekie

Dovekies are rarely seen near shore and for this reason are not familiar to most people. Dovekies are poor flyers and need stiff ocean breezes to help them become airborne. Sometimes after powerful storms, a few are driven onto beaches and even far inland. These waifs are often stranded since they are unable to take off from land and thus can't fly back to the ocean.

For anyone willing to take a really long drive and a ferry ride to see a Dovekie, there is a harbor called Bay Bulls, located on the Avalon Peninsula in Newfoundland, which is full of Dovekies every winter. The local people call Dovekies "bull birds," perhaps because of their short necks, and this is how the harbor got its name.

Every few years following late autumn or winter storms, there will be a "wreck" of Dovekies along the Atlantic coast. The birds may be picked up far inland, even in Vermont or New York state. They often land on wet or icy roads, perhaps mistaking them for water. Since they must have water and sea breezes to take off again, they become stranded and helpless. Fortunately, these disasters do not happen very often.

Dovekie in a Country Store

A birder was visiting a New England country store about 80 miles from the coast. The proprietor was a hunter who had a number of stuffed animals on display. Suddenly, the visitor noticed a small bird among the animals and recognized it as a Dovekie. Surprised, he enquired of the store owner how he happened to have a stuffed Dovekie. The owner replied that he had found the bird in his front yard one day after a violent storm. The bird appeared injured and confused, and he had nursed it back to health. When he thought it was ready, he took the Dovekie outside, and, holding it with both hands, tossed it into the air as high as he could. Unfortunately, Dovekies are very poor flyers and need a lengthy takeoff run across open water into a stiff sea breeze in order to become airborne. The poor Dovekie dropped like a rock and broke his neck on the hard ground. And that is the sad story of how the Dovekie came to be stuffed and mounted and put on display in the country store.

The Shape of Seabird Eggs

The eggs of birds which nest on the ledges of high cliffs are pointed at one end (pear-shaped) and balanced so that they are less likely to roll off the edge. If pushed or jostled, they tend to spin or roll in a tight circle and thus many wayward eggs avoid a long fall. The eggs of "hole-nesters," such as owls, whose eggs never risk a fall, are much more round. An elongated egg shape also allows for more body contact with the parent during incubation. To see how important this pointed egg shape is to seabird survival, try placing a chicken's egg on a countertop and give it a push. Notice how easily the roundish chicken egg will roll off the edge.

A Good Reason to Lay Eggs

Imagine how difficult flight would be if a female bird had to undergo pregnancy in the same manner as mammals. Bats are mammals that fly and still manage to give birth to live young, so it is not impossible. Yet, the ability to reproduce by laying eggs gives birds an advantage which may have helped them to prosper.

A Shower of Eggs

Many of the islands where murres breed are restricted as bird sanctuaries, and visitors to the colonies must obtain special permits. One reason is that the murres are easily frightened and think first of their own survival without regard for their eggs. If startled, a whole flock might panic and suddenly leap from the ledges into the air, resulting in a shower of eggs onto the rocks below.

Salt Glands

Most seabirds have special salt glands which expel the large amounts of salt taken in during their life at sea. These glands are located near the eyes and the excess salt drips out through the bill or the nostrils. Individual drops are removed with a shake of the head.

The salt gland is the secret to survival at sea where fresh drinking water does not exist. It restores the bird's normal salt balance after a sea-water drink.

Atlantic Puffin

The name puffin may refer to the fuzzy down of the young or to the puffed-out appearance of the adult bird's belly. But of course, the puffin's most outstanding feature is its outlandish, multi-colored beak which has earned it the title, "sea parrot" of the North Atlantic. This beak is especially brilliant during the summer breeding season.

The Gift of Grab

The most endearing feature of the puffin is its ability to hold a large number of fish crosswise in its beak. The feat of holding the fish already caught and still managing to catch more never fails to amaze. The secret is a row of special spines on the roof of the mouth and the tongue which holds the fish already caught while the puffin grabs for more. The favorite food of the puffin along the New England coast is the herring which occurs in vast schools. Further north, puffins are more likely to be seen with capelin in their bills (as in the photo at right).

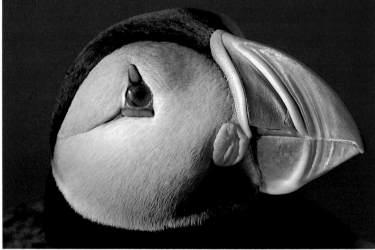

◁ The colorful parts of the beak are actually part of an outer sheath that covers the beak and is shed annually, so the puffin's appearance in winter is not so striking.

Do Seabirds Drink Fresh Water?

Although some species such as gulls regularly visit inland areas for fresh water, other species such as storm-petrels and shearwaters will not take fresh water even if it is offered. Still other species would probably prefer fresh water but do not make special trips to obtain it.

A Spectacular Fledging

As might be imagined, when it is time for the young of auk families to leave their rocky ledges and go into the sea, it is a big step down, and there is no way to ease into their new lives gradually. The young auks usually leave their ledges at night to avoid predators. Flapping their stubby wings wildly, they sail off into the darkness or clamber down over rocks to the water. Young puffins and Black Guillemots leave their nests alone, but the young of murres and Razorbills are accompanied by their fathers who stay with the youngsters at sea while they learn how to fish.

Puffins nest in burrows which they dig in the ground, although they sometimes nest in the crevices between rocks, like the guillemots. This affords protection for them and their young from their most serious predator, the Great Black-backed Gull. But they are vulnerable to mammalian predators and on islands where rats, dogs, or cats have been introduced by man, puffin populations have fallen sharply.

In former years, whole colonies were destroyed by hunters. The puffins were easily caught as they left their burrows. Some were eaten as were their eggs, and there are even stories of them being used for lobster bait! As a result, puffin populations were so reduced by the beginning of this century that there were only two nesting sites left along the Maine coast; Matinicus Rock and Machias Seal Island.

A project of the National Audubon Society recently brought puffins back to the island of Eastern Egg Rock where they had nested many years before. Baby puffins were captured off the coast of Newfoundland and placed in artificial burrows. They became imprinted with their new surroundings and later nested at their new home instead of returning to Newfoundland.

Puffins have strong legs and, unlike the other auks, can stand and run with ease. But when fully stuffed with fish, they have some difficulty in becoming airborne.

Eating Puffins

Puffins have traditionally been taken as food in Newfoundland, France, Scandinavia, and Iceland. The usual method of capture is to sweep them from the air with a net attached to a long pole. An experienced man can catch hundreds in a day by this means. These photos show puffin hunting in Iceland as it used to be. It still continues today in some places.

Prince Charles of England receives millions of dollars annually in rents from estates scattered throughout his country. Among these rents is the requirement of 300 puffins annually from his tenants in the Scilly Isles, a group of small islands off the tip of Cornwall (near Land's End, England).

Storm-Petrels

Wilson's Storm-Petrel
Leach's Storm-Petrel

Storm-petrels are the smallest of the seabirds. The word "petrel" probably comes from "Peter," a biblical reference to St. Peter. The connection to St. Peter is that storm-petrels appear to be walking on water as they feed, as St. Peter walked on the water (Matthew XIV: 29-30).

Storm-petrels fly just above the waves and snatch plankton and small fish that are near the surface of the sea. They frequently touch the water surface with their feet as they flutter along. This touching of the water surface is called "pattering," which in addition to helping the petrel stay airborne, may help the petrel stir up and corral its prey.

The "storm" in the storm-petrel's name refers to the observation that storm-petrels seek shelter from storms by flying next to ships and using them as windbreaks (although Leach's Storm-Petrel is not known to do this).

World-wide, storm-petrels may be among the most numerous birds because of their huge habitat.

Note the dark color, the forked tail, and the white, divided patch on the

Leach's Storm-Petrel

Tubenoses

"Tubenoses" are a group of birds which include storm-petrels. Tubenoses have beaks which look like they have been put together in segments or plates. Even more distinctive is the tube on top of the beak which encloses the bird's nostrils. The advantage of having the nostrils enclosed is not known, though it may be related to the function of salt glands (see page 115).

rump of Leach's Storm-Petrel. Leach's Storm-Petrel is the only tubenose that nests along our coast, from Cape Cod northward. They dig burrows in the ground or tunnel under driftwood to a depth of two or three feet. The adults take turns incubating while the other mate is far at sea feeding on the small crustaceans which make up most of its food.

The homing instinct of a storm-petrel is remarkable. It can return from 75 to 100 miles at sea and fly straight to its burrow in darkness or dense fog. Because of the nocturnal habits of this species, it is seldom observed.

Wilson's Storm-Petrels

Mother Carrie's Chickens

Storm-Petrels have been called Mother Carrie's Chickens and fishermen often abbreviate this to Kerrychick. There are several possible origins for this name. One suggestion is that it comes from Madre Cara, "dear mother," the plaintive cry of worried Italian sailors during storms. Another idea is that Mother Carrie is the aunt of Davey Jones, the fictional character who welcomed drowned sailors to the sea bottom. A third possibility is that the name Mother Carrie is a corrupted form of Virgin Mary.

Kittiwake

Black-legged Kittiwake

Kittiwakes are gulls, but are quite different from other gull species. Except for a few months of summer when they nest on the cliff ledges of the coastal islands, they spend their lives at sea. They are the most oceanic and the most northern of the gulls in the Northeast. They are rarely seen inland even during winter although they may be found off the coast.

The name "kittiwake" imitates their cries. "Black-legged" distinguishes them from Red-legged Kittiwakes, a similar species found on the west coast. In New England kittiwakes are also called Winter Gulls or Frost Gulls because of their arrival offshore in the fall.

Kittiwakes build sturdy, compact nests composed of mud reinforced with seaweed, grasses, and other debris. They mold the materials together with their feet. If their nesting islands lack mud, kittiwakes go to the mainland in mud-collecting parties.

Seabird Hot-spots

1. Bonaventure Island in the Gulf of St. Lawrence near the tip of the Gaspé Peninsula in Quebec has large seabird colonies including the largest nesting colony of Gannets. Boats from the town of Perce take visitors to the island daily. July and August are best. 2. The Avalon Peninsula in Newfoundland is a real treasure for birders. The Witless Bay Sanctuary features puffins and storm-petrels. There are three islands in the sanctuary, including the largest, Gull Island. Bay Bulls Harbor is part of Witless Bay and features Dovekies in winter as well as sea ducks, including thousands of eiders. Cape St. Mary's has gannet nesting colonies on coastal cliffs plus kittiwakes and murres. 3. Grand Manan Island in New Brunswick (in the Bay of Fundy just north of the Maine border) has puffin colonies. 4. So do several islands off the Maine coast such as Matinicus Rock and Eastern Egg Rock. 5. Machias Seal Island has puffins and guillemots. Boats can be hired to view the nesting colonies from the water.

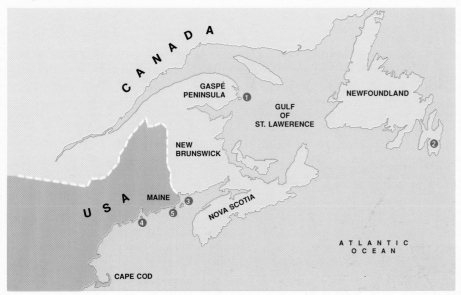

Seabird-watching Expeditions

The best places for viewing seabirds are the Canada coastal provinces (the Maritimes) and several places in Maine (Eastern Egg Rock, Matinicus Rock, and Matinicus Island). Many of the best islands are only open to visitors with special permits and are accessible only under ideal weather conditions.

Permits are often required and tightly controlled because people landing on these islands could disturb nesting birds and could easily destroy a whole season's nesting. However, there are boat trips available from many points along the New England coast. One notable trip is aboard the Bluenose, an automobile ferry which sails daily from Bar Harbor, Maine to Yarmouth, Nova Scotia. There are also trips on car ferries from Portland to Yarmouth which result in many seabird sightings.

Many private charter boat tours of the bird islands operate from Newfoundland and cater to tourists. These tours give birders a view of the nesting islands from the sea without disturbing the birds.

Waterbird Hot-Spots

This map is just an overview of the most famous and spectacular birding locations. There is good birding in almost every area. The local Audubon Society can help the beginner contact friendly birders who know the best places. Each state in the Northeast has enough good birding locations to fill a book, and in fact many such books have been published.

3. Acadia National Park, Maine
This beautiful park features ducks and loons in winter.

1 & 2. Eastport, Maine (at the northern border of Maine).
Strong tides create a large whirlpool which is visible from the docks at Eastport. This whirlpool stirs up food from the ocean bottom which, for about two weeks in the fall, attracts as many as 100,000 phalaropes.

Lubec, Maine
There are miles of mudflats which attract huge numbers of migrating shorebirds in September.

4. Isle au Haut, near Bar Harbor, Maine
This is the place to see migrating Harlequin Ducks in spring.

5. Monehegan Island, Maine
The island is accessible by ferry from Port Clyde and is a good place to see migratory birds in spring and fall.

PORTLAND•

6 & 7. Ried State Park near Brunswick, Maine
This location is good for shorebirds, also Red-throated Loons and mergansers in winter. The beach is unusual for the area because it is sandy rather than rocky. Lots of ducks can be seen near the mouth of the Kennebec River.

Marymeeting Bay near Bath, Maine
This is a traditional duck-hunting area which attracts huge numbers of waterfowl. Almost every species of duck and goose of the Northeast can be seen here in spring and fall.

15. Cornell University Laboratory of Ornithology, Ithaca, NY
Sapsucker Woods Sanctuary features small ponds that attract waterfowl. There are nature trails, a visitor's center, and a bird observatory.

9. Block Island, Rhode Island
Block Island is best in fall, poor in spring. The Columbus Day weekend is the peak of the migration season here and many birding tours are planned for these few days. Numerous geese and waterfowl maybe seen as well as cormorants.

BOSTON•

8. Cape Cod
This is a mecca for tourists, especially in summer and tends to be crowded, but is good for birds at any season. It includes the Cape Cod National Seashore which offers birders a spectacular mix of upland and beaches. A notable attraction is the Monomoy National Wildlife Refuge near Chatham. This former peninsula is now broken up into islands which are known for gatherings of shorebird migrants (late spring and fall) and concentrations of landbird migrants in fall. There are also major colonies of Herring and Great Black-backed Gulls.

11. Sandy Hook, New Jersey and Central Park, New York City
Sandy Hook is an undeveloped piece of land in an urban sea which acts as an "oasis" style trap for migrants passing New York City and New Jersey. Large concentrations may occur. It is better in the spring than the fall. Central park is another "oasis" for migrating birds. Nocturnal migrants that find themselves over New York City at dawn see nothing but concrete jungle. They naturally head for the only spot of green and large "fallouts" (concentrations of migrating birds) are possible.

NEW YORK CITY

PHILADELPHIA•

10. Montauk Point
As a point of land sticking out into the sea farther than the surrounding land, Montauk gets more than its share of migrants.

12. Brigantine National Wildlife Refuge, New Jersey
About an hour's drive north of Cape May, this hot-spot features a lengthy automobile trail along dykes constructed through a large wetlands area. This refuge is especially noted for shorebirds (July through October) and waterfowl (October through April). Thousands of Snow Geese appear in late fall. The Atlantic City skyline is visible in the distance.

BALTIMORE•

WASHINGTON, D.C.•

13. Cape May, New Jersey
Cape May is the tip of a funnel formed by a peninsula of land in the middle of the Atlantic Flyway. This land funnel concentrates birds during the fall migration. Cape May is on the shores of the Delaware Bay and is the major staging area for Red Knots and other shorebirds that are migrating north in spring.

14. Bombay Hook National Wildlife Refuge, Dover, Delaware
Bombay Hook is a large reserve of tidal marshes, plus various other habitats.